THE GNR & I
DONCA

A4 No. 4500
Class A4 4-6-2 locomotive No. 4500, *Sir Ronald Matthews*, is pictured at Doncaster Works during April 1939. It had just been renamed after the LNER chairman and received steel, cut-out numbers on the cab and metal LNER letters on the tender. The locomotive was built in April 1938 and originally named *Garganey* with transfer numbers and letters being applied, which were gold with red shading. No. 4500 (later BR No. 60001) spent its entire career operating from Gateshead shed, leaving service in October 1964, and was subsequently scrapped.

Locomotive Drawing Office Staff on VE Day
The Doncaster Works Locomotive Drawing Office staff pose for a group photograph on VE Day, 7 May 1945.

THE GNR & LNER IN DONCASTER

PETER TUFFREY

AMBERLEY

No. 6701 *Tommy*
In the 1930s plans were produced to electrify the railway line between Manchester, Sheffield and Wath using a 1,500-volt DC overhead system. These plans stalled because of the outbreak of the Second World War but the construction of a locomotive designed to run on the line continued. Pictured is the prototype locomotive, No. 6701, which was designed by Sir Nigel Gresley and built at Doncaster in 1940. It was tested on the Manchester South Junction and Altrincham Railway in 1941 but then went into storage for the duration of the war. In September 1947 the Netherlands Railway allowed the locomotive to be extensively tested by the LNER. It returned to England in 1952, renumbered by BR to 26000 and was also named *Tommy* after the nickname given to it by the Dutch. The original proposed electrified route opened in 1954 and fifty-seven more locomotives were built to the design at Gorton. *Tommy* was withdrawn in 1970.

First published 2013

Amberley Publishing
The Hill, Stroud
Gloucestershire, GL5 4EP

www.amberley-books.com

British Library Cataloguing in Publication Data.
A catalogue record for this book is available from the British Library.

ISBN 978 1 4456 0125 0

Typeset in 10pt on 12pt Sabon.
Typesetting and Origination by Amberley Publishing.
Printed in the UK.

Contents

Crimpsall Roof View, Late 1940s
A view from Crimpsall Repair Shop roof. The building straight ahead is the Iron Foundry, while to the right is the New Weigh House and behind that is the Paint Shop. After the demise of steam the Iron Foundry became the Crane and Chain Repair Shop. The Crimpsall Repair Shop was reorganised to repair diesel locomotives, but in 2008 it was demolished and the site is to accommodate new housing.

Acknowledgements

I am grateful to the following people for their help: Miriam Burrell, Hugh Parkin and Derek Porter.

Special thanks to my son, Tristram Tuffrey, for his help with research on the text.

This book is dedicated to the memory of Malcolm Crawley

Introduction

The days of the Great Northern Railway and the London & North Eastern Railway are probably the greatest in Doncaster's history, extending from the early 1840s to December 1947. From the 1840s the town became a major point on the new railway system and a little later it was to have a large say in the production and maintenance of railway transport, i.e. building and repairing locomotives, carriages and wagons.

Yet to kick-start it all, and bring about Doncaster's first industrial revolution, help was needed from Doncaster MP Edmund Becket Denison. With great efforts he persuaded the Great Northern Railway to extend their London–York railway route through the town, instead of avoiding it by travelling via Lincoln, Gainsborough and Selby.

Once Doncaster was firmly placed on the line, Denison wasted no time in coaxing the GNR to transfer their main locomotive repair works from Boston to Doncaster.

By 1853, the Works, or the Plant as it is more commonly known, covered approximately 11 acres. Initially, the work carried out there included the maintenance of locomotives, carriages and wagons, but eventually the site began building, first carriages and eventually locomotives. Doncaster GNR was also involved with works belonging to the NER and NBR in the building and repairing of carriages for the East Coast Joint Stock. Later in the nineteenth century, wagon building and repair would be transferred to a site approximately 2 miles south of the Plant.

Locomotive building at Doncaster began in 1867 with Patrick Stirling designing a Class F2 engine, and it could not have been predicted then that he was beginning a great tradition that would bring international fame for Doncaster. In time Stirling designed the 4-2-2 express passenger engines that were fondly known as 'Eight-Footers' or 'Singles'. This was because of their 8-foot driving wheels and they played an important part in the 'Race to the North'.

Carriage building predated that of locomotives and, throughout the remainder of the nineteenth century, vehicles were built for the ECJS and the GNR at Doncaster under several carriage superintendents, most notably E. F. Howlden.

By the turn of the century the Doncaster Carr locomotive shed was well established and expansion took place on the Plant site to include the building of the vast Crimpsall Workshops.

When Stirling died suddenly in office during 1895, the task of designing and building more powerful steam engines was taken up by Henry A. Ivatt. Under his guidance the 4-4-2 'Atlantic' express passenger engine was produced at the Plant. The first of these, No. 990, named *Henry Oakley* after a GNR general manager, is now preserved as part of the national collection.

In the early years of the twentieth century, one man came along, Nigel Gresley, who would alter the course of carriage and locomotive building and firmly place Doncaster's name in the history of railways forever. He started as carriage and wagon superintendent at Doncaster in 1905, and while holding this post introduced many new features to the GNR and ECJS rolling stock.

When Gresley succeeded Ivatt as locomotive superintendent in the autumn of 1911 he embarked on a course that would produce some of the most outstanding steam locomotives ever seen. One of these was the Pacific, or 4-6-2, engine, the first of which was built at Doncaster in 1922, and this may be regarded as the pinnacle of GNR locomotive design.

A year later, following grouping and the emergence of the LNER, Gresley moved to offices in London, along with hand-picked Doncaster staff, to head the company's locomotive and carriage department. Gresley kept a close link with Doncaster throughout the remainder of the 1920s and into the 1930s. In fact during the latter decade Doncaster Works and Gresley enjoyed some of their finest achievements in carriage and wagon building. Mostly notably the Plant produced Gresley's A4 locomotives including *Mallard* and a number of his unique carriage sets among them the Coronation train.

I have attempted to feature a number of Gresley's finest works in this book, along with those of his predecessors. Not least are the workforces of both the GNR and LNER and efforts have been made to illustrate them in their many tasks. Women at work at the Plant in both world wars are also featured.

The illustrations are from a number of sources including ex-Works official photographer Ben Burrell, as well as the collections of Derek Porter and Hugh Parkin. Ben Burrell's list of Doncaster Works photographs proved particularly useful.

Sadly, the important role Doncaster once played in the country's rail network is now lost, perhaps forever. The Plant Works site and work has drastically contracted, with housing set to be built on the area once occupied by the Crimpsall Workshops. But, hopefully this book will go some way to illustrate and record the glorious past of the GNR and LNER in Doncaster.

1

The Great Northern Railway and the East Coast Joint Stock

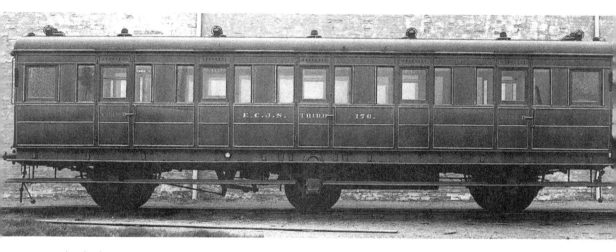

Third-Class Corridor Carriage No. 176

The use of four and six wheels for the East Coast Joint Stock was a regular feature of the design throughout the latter part of the nineteenth century until the introduction of bogies in 1893. However, even with the introduction of bogie stock, six-wheel vehicles were still being produced until around 1896. This third-class corridor vehicle, produced at Doncaster Works in 1891, was among the final six to be produced to the design. Six and four had been produced in the previous two years respectively. The carriages comprised five compartments: one for ladies, two standard thirds and two gentlemen's smoking compartments. Toilets were also provided at either end of the carriage. No. 176 was part of the ECJS until September 1922 when it was transferred to GNR stock.

East Coast Third-Class Carriage No. 252

Carriage construction at Doncaster Works predated locomotive erection by almost a decade when it began in the mid-1850s. Doncaster had a long association with the manufacture of the East Coast Joint Stock (which included contributions from the GNR/NER/NBR) and this had started in the early 1860s. Built at Doncaster in 1896, this vehicle was one of three built to the diagram 28 design (1909 Diagram Book). It is an open third-class carriage, 65 feet and 5¼ inches long with a clerestory roof and twelve wheels split onto two bogies. The carriage was in service for thirty years and was withdrawn in 1926.

Third-Class Dining Saloon Interior

Pictured around 1895 is an East Coast Joint Stock third-class dining saloon. Although the ECJS first appeared in the early 1860s, it was not until the early 1890s that dining facilities were provided for passengers travelling on the main line between London King's Cross and Edinburgh. This third-class dining saloon was one of four built at Doncaster in 1894 to replace ones built in 1893 after they were found to be too luxurious and drawing the first-class passengers away from the first-class saloons. The seating in the new saloons was increased from twenty-four to forty-two. They also had the design of the roof altered to include clerestories, which ran the length of the carriage roof. All four of the third-class dining saloons survived until after grouping and were withdrawn between February 1926 and February 1927.

First-Class Dining Saloon No. 332

This vehicle was one of four first-class dining saloons built at Doncaster during 1902 to the diagram 77 design (diagram 55 in the 1903 Diagram Book). Seating was for sixteen, split evenly between smoking and non-smoking compartments. The seats were arranged in sets of two facing each other. The rest of the dining saloon accommodated the kitchen and a pantry. The carriage is seen after 1914 when the small windows had been replaced with a larger type and the seating had risen to eighteen. No. 332 was removed from service in September 1937.

Six-Wheel Brake No. 259

This six-wheel brake van, No. 259, was one of three constructed at Doncaster in 1896 to the diagram 41 design (1909 Diagram Book). The vehicle also has the distinction of being among the last five vehicles (all brake vans) fitted with six wheels. No. 259 was 32 feet long and 8 feet 10 inches wide and the interior offered very little in terms of fittings. Two shelves, a letter rack and cupboard were provided but the rest of the space was allocated to passengers' luggage, which tended to be large in volume on the Anglo-Scottish services. This brake van was disposed of to the North British Railway in October 1922.

Compartment Third-Class Carriage No. 58

Built at Doncaster in 1903, this eight-wheeled vehicle comprised seven compartments for third-class passengers and could seat forty-two. One toilet was provided between the standard and the smoking compartments. The length of the body was 53 feet 6⅝ inches and it was 8 feet 6 inches wide. A corridor 2 feet wide ran the length of the body and it had four dummy doors placed on that side. After leaving the ECJS the carriage was transferred to the GN during August 1925 and renumbered 41694.

Composite Dining Saloon No. 352

Composite Dining Saloon No. 352 comprised a first-class dining saloon, kitchen, pantries and third-class dining saloon. It was built at Doncaster along with three others in 1905 and these were the last saloons to be built with clerestory roofs and two six-wheel bogies. The first-class saloon seated twelve and the third-class seated eighteen. The two saloons were split by the kitchen, which measured 11 feet 3¼ inches long, and the two pantries were placed either side measuring 5 feet 11 inches and 4 feet 10 inches respectively. The saloon was transferred to Scotland in January 1929 and renumbered 32453.

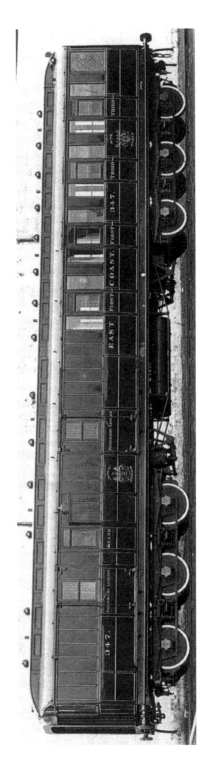

Brake/First/Third Composite No. 347

No. 347 was built in 1903 but not in the form seen here. It originally appeared from Doncaster as a brake/third-class vehicle. In 1904 it was rebuilt to include accommodation for first-class passengers. The carriage measured 61 feet long and was 8 feet wide with four compartments and a lavatory at one end; a corridor 2 feet wide connected the compartments. This particular carriage was damaged beyond repair by a fire while at Wallyford in 1909 and was replaced by a carriage carrying the same number. This differed in appearance to the original as it had a semi-elliptical roof and the number of wheels was reduced to eight. Both carriages had some bad fortune while in service; the original was damaged at Grantham in 1906 and the replacement was withdrawn after sustaining damage at Retford in February 1923.

Brake/Third Class No. 97

No. 97 was among ten vehicles built at Doncaster Works in 1908 to the diagram 49 design for a third-class/brake carriage. It was constructed with a semi-elliptical roof and a body measuring 58 feet 6 inches long on two bogies with four wheels each. Space was provided in six compartments for thirty-six seats and 16 feet of the carriage was allocated to the brake section. In 1914 No. 97 and another carriage were modified by having three compartments removed to accommodate further space for the brake section. This alteration led to the reclassification of the design to diagram 49A. No. 97 was transferred to the GC section in October 1935 and renumbered to 52092.

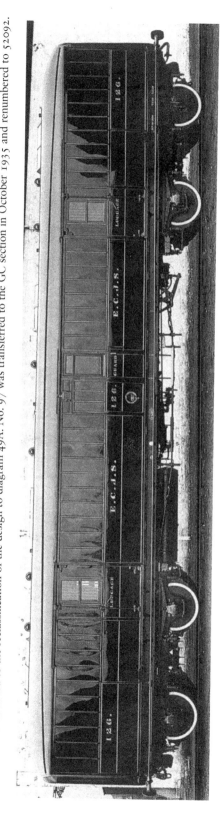

Brake No. 126

A major turning point in carriage construction for the ECJS occurred in 1905 when H. N. Gresley became carriage and wagon superintendent of the GNR. He replaced E. F. Howlden, who had held the position for almost thirty years. Gresley moved to modernise the basic design of the vehicles to include a semi-elliptical roof, curved side sheets, four-wheel bogie, steel underframes and improved riding. This was implemented first for the GN and then the ECJS with an order for new and replacement stock in 1906. No. 126 was the prototype brake van and produced at Doncaster to the diagram 39 design. The carriage was renumbered by the LNER in October 1925 as No. 110 and was later transferred to the GN section where it acquired No. 4037.

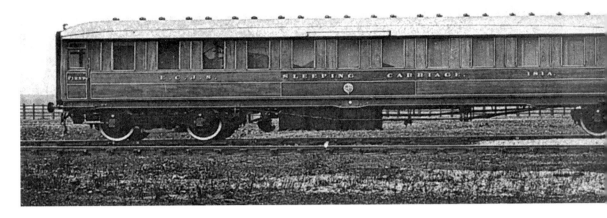

Above: **Articulated Twin Sleeper Carriages Nos 181A and 181**
The first articulated coaching stock appeared in 1907 utilising coach bodies that had been built in the Howlden era. Due to budget restrictions, replacing these carriages was not viable and it was decided to attach them to articulated bogies. Formerly mounted on six wheels, only minor modifications were needed to mount the bodies to the standard 8-foot bogie. This not only made savings but improved the riding, reduced the weight and improved safety. Further articulated stock appeared in the following years consisting of two, three and even four coaches. Nos 181 and 181A, twin sleeping cars, were built new at Doncaster in 1922 at a cost of over £12,600. The cars had twenty berths and were noted at the time for their modern design. The carriages were later renumbered by the LNER as 1181 and 1182.

Opposite page, bottom: **Royal Saloon No. 395 Under Construction**
Taken on 9 November 1907 at Doncaster Works this image depicts the construction of Royal Saloon No. 395 (the King's saloon). Two carriages were commissioned in 1906 as no dedicated ECJS stock existed for journeys by King Edward VII and Queen Alexandra. The carriages were constructed at Doncaster and York (No. 396), both vehicles costing £7,000 to build. The exterior was the same on both, however the interior layout differed with the Queen's carriage having more compartments and a corridor. The bodies were 67 feet long, made from Javan teak and had fish-belly underframes.

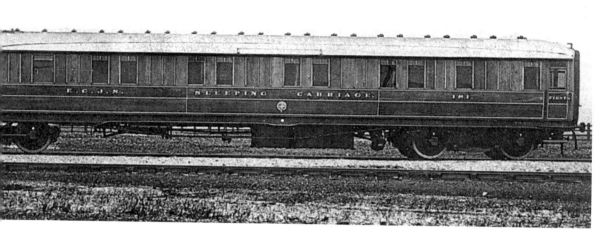

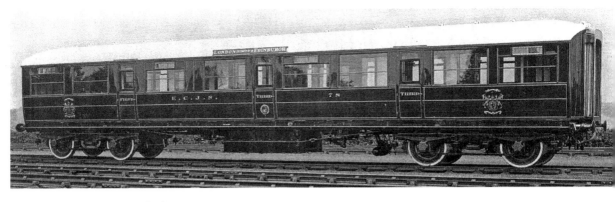

Composite Vehicle No. 78

Composite vehicle No. 78, Doncaster-built in 1914, could accommodate first- and third-class passengers, having two first- and four third-class compartments.

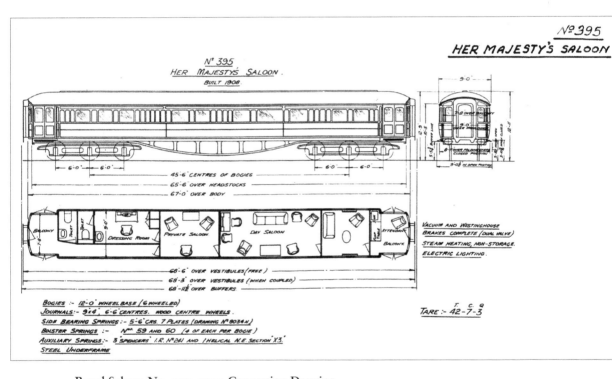

Royal Saloon No. 395, 1924 Conversion Drawing

After grouping the LNER refurbished both royal saloons, changing the layout of the carriages and their use, with No. 395 becoming the Queen's Saloon. The dressing room was shortened with a corridor utilising the space and the bedroom was removed and became a private room. The fixtures and fittings were also modernised. The carriages remained in use until 1978 and both carriages were subsequently preserved with No. 395 housed at the National Railway Museum.

2
Great Northern Railway Carriages

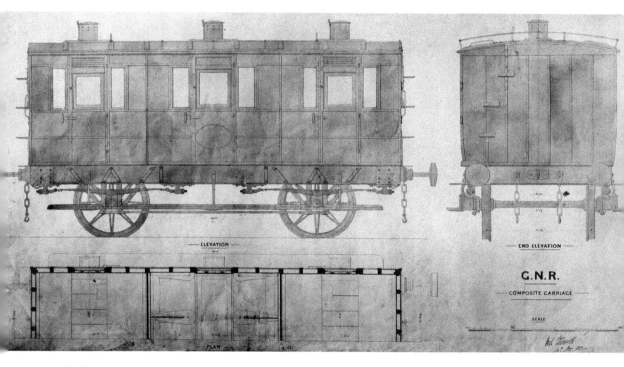

GNR Composite Carriage Drawing, 1853
This GNR composite carriage was designed in 1853. It was 18 feet 1 inch long, had three compartments and four wheels and was a standard design for carriages in the 1850s and 1860s.

Prince of Wales Saloon No. 1691

Seen here is the interior of the GNR Royal Saloon carriage, built at Doncaster in 1876 for the Prince of Wales. It was constructed to the design of Patrick Stirling, the GNR locomotive superintendent, and used two four-wheel bogies. No. 1691 was constructed because the Prince of Wales complained that the previous carriage provided by the GNR was unsatisfactory. It was to be replaced in 1888 but the new carriage again proved unsuitable and No. 1691 remained in use until the beginning of the twentieth century.

GNR Third-Class Carriage No. 85

Pictured at Doncaster Works in April 1910 is a GNR third-class carriage with six wheels. It was built there in 1890 to the design of E. F. Howlden, carriage and wagon superintendent. The vehicle measured 32 feet 1½ inches long, 7 feet 9 inches wide and 11 feet 7⅝ inches high. Five compartments were provided for third-class passengers, each seating ten and measuring 6 feet 3 inches by 7 feet 9 inches. No. 85 became No. 485 after grouping and left service in 1938.

GNR Third-Class Dining Saloon No. 2839

This carriage was built at Doncaster in 1898 based on the design of the ECJS dining saloon. It was built to be part of trains running between King's Cross and Yorkshire but later worked on services between London and Manchester. No. 2839 provided seating for forty-two third-class passengers in three compartments. Two sections seated twelve (one section was designated smoking), while the

First-Class Semi-Dining Carriage No. 312

This photograph, taken in April 1900, shows first-class dining saloon/compartment carriage No. 312. At one end of the 59-foot 8⅝-inch body were two first-class dining compartments seating eight and four respectively. Four first-class compartments then followed with two lavatories at either end of the compartments. A corridor connected the compartments to the dining saloon.

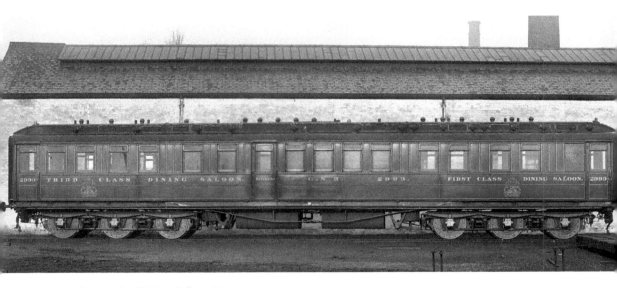

Composite Dining Saloon No. 2993

This carriage was similar in design to the three ECJS composite dining carriages introduced in 1900, however the interior layout was slightly altered. First-class seating was reduced from twelve to eight to make space for the inclusion of a second pantry. The kitchen was enlarged slightly to 11 feet 7¼ inches from the 10-foot 2¼-inch kitchen of the ECJS vehicles. The exterior appearance was the same as they both had twelve wheels and a clerestory roof. The weight of the GNR carriage was increased by about 3 tons to 41 tons 2 cwt. A larger composite dining saloon was introduced for the ECJS in 1905 and had the same kitchen and pantry layout as No. 2993, but the new carriages had increased seating. This image of No. 2993 was taken in February 1904.

Carriage Department Staff, 1909

Carriage construction started at Doncaster in the mid-1850s under the direction of John Coffin. The facilities for building carriages at this time consisted of two buildings; one was located in the building facing Doncaster station and the other, a larger building, was located behind the first, adjoining the wagon shop. By the time of this photograph in 1909 the facilities had increased with the carriage shop extending into the wagon shop and two new buildings being added. The West Carriage Shop and North Carriage Shed were built around 1897.

Carriage Department Staff, 1910

More Carriage Department staff pose for the camera *c.* 1910. The men in the middle of the group wearing bowler hats are the Carriage Shop foremen. Note how young the boys in the front row are.

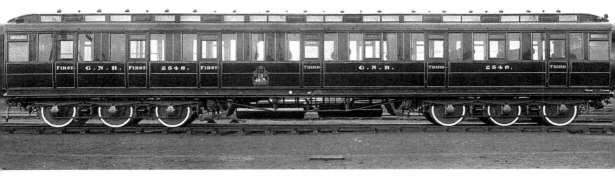

GNR First/Third Composite No. 2548

The interior layout of this carriage is interesting as it uses both compartments and open seating. Two open third-class sections were provided measuring 10 feet 9 inches by 8 feet 6 inches and 16 feet 2 inches by 8 feet 6 inches with seating for eighteen and fifteen respectively. Three compartments were for first-class passengers with four passengers to a compartment. Seven carriages, including No. 2543, were built in 1905 to this design, which was designated diagram 248H by the GNR.

GNR Third Class No. 3127

Seen from the compartment side on 17 July 1909 is GNR third-class corridor carriage No. 3127. This vehicle was one of five carriages built to the diagram 228 design in 1909. Seven compartments were provided in the body, which measured 52 feet 6 inches by 8 feet 6 inches. Three of the compartments were designated smoking and two toilets were provided at either end of the vehicle. Seating was for forty-two passengers. The total weight of this carriage was 27 tons 14 cwt.

Carriage Shop, *c.* 1912
A view inside Doncaster Works. Note that the vehicles are in various stages of construction.

GNR First-Class Dining Saloon No. 3250
Pictured on 30 October 1912 is the interior of GNR first-class dining saloon No. 3250. It was one of four built between 1912 and 1914 to the design of H. N. Gresley. The carriage was 52 feet 6 inches long and 9 feet wide, supported by two 8-foot 6-inch bogies. This view is taken from the entrance to the vehicle and captures the dining saloon with the kitchen located at the other end. Seating was for eighteen; three groups of four and three of two at the tables, which were made from mahogany and have been left undecorated for this photograph.

Above: **GNR Triplet No. 2636**
Following the introduction of articulated coaches into the ECJS, the GNR went about converting more old coaching stock to articulated sets for use on shorter-distance services. By 1915 thirteen sets of three coaches were in service and the sets comprised a composite brake/third and two composite first/third carriages. The total length of the set was 108 feet 4 inches. Each carriage consisted of five compartments and seating was provided for 100 third-class and 24 first-class passengers.

Opposite page, bottom: **War Women and Composite Carriage No. 1299**
Pictured in Doncaster Works' North Carriage Shed during the First World War are women workers cleaning composite GNR carriage No. 1299. This vehicle comprised six wheels and five compartments; two first class and three third that could seat twelve and thirty respectively. As the war progressed women found themselves increasingly employed in the various spheres of operations at Doncaster. Another task they were employed on was the preparation of 6-inch high-explosive artillery shells.

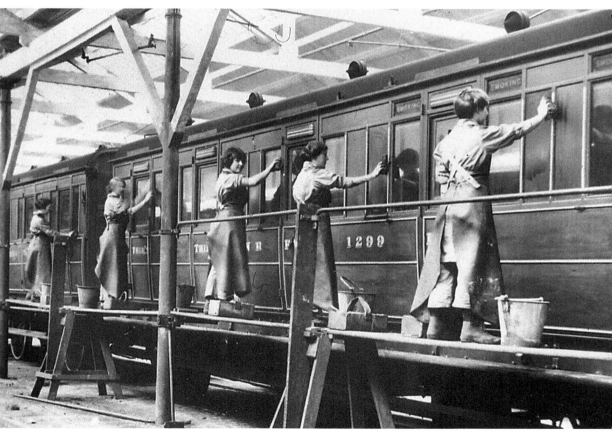

West Carriage Shop, *c.* 1916
A busy scene in the West Carriage Shop at Doncaster Works *c.* 1916. Repairs and maintenance are being carried out on Howlden-era six-wheel coaches in the background and in the foreground on No. 3047, an example of Gresley's Sheffield

stock. The stock was made up of three trains and was introduced in 1906 for the services between King's Cross and Manchester and Sheffield. No. 3047 is an example of an open third-class carriage, which could seat forty-two.

Above: **Carriage Repairs**
A view inside the West Carriage Shop *c.* 1916. On the left, attention is being given to a third-class coach.

Opposite page, top: **Women War Workers**
On 18 July 1916 female workers are seen cleaning an open third-class carriage at Doncaster.

Opposite page, bottom: **Women War Workers Cleaning Carriage No. 324**
In July 1916 a number of pictures were taken at Doncaster Works to document the important contribution that women were making to the work being undertaken. The scene captured here in the West Carriage Shop yard shows the cleaning of ECJS brake/third carriage No. 324. It was built at Doncaster in 1902 to diagram 54 and was in service for over thirty years, being withdrawn in December 1933. After the war, H. N. Gresley praised the efforts of the women employed at Doncaster Works during the conflict commenting that he could not speak highly enough of their adaptability in undertaking new tasks.

Leeds Quintuplet Set Nos 9011–9015

The Leeds Quintuplet Set was built at Doncaster between 1920 and 1921 for the King's Cross–Leeds and return service. Costing just over £17,000, the set had five coaches; a brake first, first-class dining saloon, kitchen carriage, third-class dining saloon and brake third; six 8-foot 6-inch bogies were used. The carriage interiors were simply decorated and they had a total seating capacity of

128. One interesting feature of the set was that it used electric cooking equipment as opposed to gas, which had been used previously in the kitchen cars. While at either King's Cross or Leeds stations the equipment drew its electricity supply from the mains at the station and once on the move batteries were used, which were charged from dynamos on the axles. The set was withdrawn after a small accident in 1953.

Woodmen
A portrait of the carpenters working at the Doncaster Carriage Works.

3
Great Northern Railway Locomotives

First Locomotive Built at Doncaster, 1868
F2 Class 0-4-2 locomotive No. 18, designed by Stirling, was the first locomotive to be built by Doncaster Works. It went to traffic in January 1868 to work either passenger services or heavy goods trains. The success of the design led to further examples being produced, the total number of which stood at 154 when the last (No. 960) entered service from Doncaster in September 1897. Fifty of these had been constructed by Sharp, Stewart & Co. and Kitson & Co. No. 18 was among the first members of the class to be withdrawn, leaving service in January 1903.

Above left: **Edmund Beckett Denison,** *c.* 1865
Edmund Beckett Denison played an important role in bringing railways to Doncaster. As MP for the town, he campaigned for the GNR to bring their new railway route through the town instead of via Lincoln, Gainsborough and Selby. Denison argued that the new railway line should follow the route of the Great North Road and to follow any other would dismiss the route used on journeys between the North and South for the last 2,000 years.

Above right: **Patrick Stirling,** *c.* 1870
Patrick Stirling was born in Kilmarnock during 1820, the first child of a large family that would have strong connections with engineering and locomotive engineering. His first job as a locomotive superintendent was for a small line in Scotland before spending thirteen years with the Glasgow & South Western Railway. In 1866 Stirling moved to the GNR and brought locomotive construction to Doncaster Works. During his time in office 709 locomotives were built to his design with further older engines being rebuilt to his specifications. Stirling died suddenly while still locomotive superintendent in 1895 and was succeeded by H. A. Ivatt.

Opposite page, top: **Henry Alfred Ivatt**
Henry Alfred Ivatt was born on 16 September 1851 in Wentworth, Cambridgeshire, and was educated at Liverpool College. He became the chief Mechanical Engineer of the Great Northern Railway in 1896, succeeding Patrick Stirling, and held the position to 1911. His son George Ivatt was also a locomotive engineer and post-war CME of the London, Midland & Scottish Railway. H. A. Ivatt died on 25 October 1923.

Opposite page, bottom: **Stirling 2-4-0 No. 755**
A group of men pose in front of Stirling's 2-4-0 locomotive No. 755. The engine was built at Doncaster Works as part of the 206 series in November 1886. This latter series had minor differences from the other 2-4-0s, which were also split into different series depending on detail variations they included when built. No. 755 was one of a number of Stirling 2-4-0s rebuilt by Ivatt; this occurred in August 1904. The locomotive was put to work for a further eighteen years before it was withdrawn in February 1923.

Stirling Single No. 548, *c.* 1878

GNR No. 548 was one of ten Stirling 'Singles' built between 1877 and 1880; it went into service in May 1878. The cost of these ten engines, without tenders, came to £2,163. No. 548 had a 4-foot ½-inch-diameter boiler, 109-square-foot firebox heating surface, boiler pressure of 140 lb per square inch and tractive effort of 11,130 lb. Later examples of Stirling Singles were to have these features increased in order to achieve a higher power output to haul the increasingly heavy trains of the time. While this proved successful to an extent, certain problems did arise due to the higher power and mechanical failures were common for these locomotives. At the turn of the century No. 548 was selected for trials with different types of spark arresters, all of which proved unsuccessful. The locomotive was removed from service in September 1904.

Stirling 4-2-2 Single No. 778
Built in November 1887, No. 778 was the final engine completed in a batch of eight 4-2-2 Singles built between November 1884 and 1887. A feature of some of these engines is the replacement of wrought iron with steel in the construction of the frames and boilers, which reduced the construction cost by approximately £200–£300 per engine. Further modifications on these engines included changes to the frames, cab, chimney and bogie. Pictured at Doncaster Works, No. 778 was withdrawn in June 1904.

Tender Shop Steam Traverser, *c*. 1892

A scene in the old Tender Shop at Doncaster Works *c*. 1892. The shop was built during a series of alterations and additions during the early 1860s. Space for the shop was found between the old Boiler Shop and the Erecting Shop, which had previously been an alleyway between the two buildings, and it was formed by building a roof over the area. On the steam traverser in the old tender shop is Stirling 2-2-2 locomotive No. 215, built at Doncaster in October 1869, and withdrawn in October 1907.

Ivatt 2-4-0 No. 1070, *c*. 1897

The first GNR 2-4-0s appeared in 1867 and were designed by Stirling with more being built until his death. Ivatt produced a further ten and these examples incorporated some different features from Stirling's locomotives. The ten Ivatt engines were built at Doncaster, starting in February 1897 and finishing in April with the completion of No. 1070. These engines had a 4-foot 5-inch boiler with a dome, a larger cab with flat top, springs above the running plate and boiler pressure was increased to 170 lb per square inch However, the safety valve cover was the same brass type that was favoured by Stirling and fitted to his examples. No. 1070 was withdrawn by the LNER in June 1924 only to be put back into service as No. 4070 in July giving a further three years' service before finally being withdrawn in May 1927.

Ivatt 0-6-0ST No. 1210, 1897

Prior to Stirling becoming GNR locomotive superintendent, saddle tank locomotives had been rebuilt from other forms of engines. Stirling appreciated the advantages of this type of locomotive and sought to standardise a design for a saddle tank. Upon Ivatt's appointment he continued the Stirling design but made his own modifications such as the use of a domed boiler, which was larger in diameter than the Stirling saddle tanks, a larger cab and a plain safety valve casing. Between 1897 and 1909, eighty-five examples of Ivatt's design were produced by Doncaster, R. Stephenson & Co. and Sharp, Stewart & Co. No. 1210 was the last of the first batch produced at Doncaster and was completed in October 1897. It survived into BR days and was withdrawn in November 1955.

Ivatt A4 No. 266, 1898

No. 266 was the prototype engine Ivatt produced for hauling GNR express passenger services. It followed Stirling's practice of employing two large-diameter driving wheels for GNR passenger engines. Consequently, twelve were produced before the wheel arrangement was abandoned by Ivatt in favour of coupled driving wheels. No. 266 was built at Doncaster in October 1898, almost two years before further examples were built with slight modifications after this prototype was fully evaluated. The alterations included increasing the diameter of the cylinders, length of the frames, size of the cab and modifying the motion. No. 266 was later classified A4 and the other engines A5. All were withdrawn in December 1917.

C2 No. 1013, 1898

No. 1013 is an example of Ivatt's C2 Class 4-4-2T locomotive design, which was constructed between 1898 and 1907; the class eventually totalled sixty. The first ten were built for working local services but the later C2s were put to work on the London suburban services. No. 1013 was built at Doncaster Works in May 1898 as part of the first batch of ten, all of which went to Leeds and Bradford to work local services, with No. 1013 spending time at both places. The C2s became LNER C12 Class after grouping and found themselves more widely dispersed and at work on different duties from what had originally been intended. No. 1013 (as BR No. 67352) was withdrawn from Grantham in November 1958.

No. 1345 in the Crimpsall Repair Shop, *c.* 1900

Lifted aloft in the Crimpsall Repair Shop is Ivatt D2 Class 4-4-0 locomotive No. 1345, erected at Doncaster in December 1898. The lift is being performed by a 55-ton crane supplied by Craven Brothers of Manchester. The D2 Class were used on secondary passenger duties and replaced Stirling-designed 2-4-0s. A total of fifty-one were built to the D2 design (also known as the 400 Class) between 1896 and 1899. The majority of these engines later became D3 Class after being rebuilt with a Gresley 4-foot 8-inch diameter boiler, with No. 1345 being so treated in February 1917. Withdrawal from service came in January 1949.

No. 990 with Driver and Fireman T. Stanley, *c.* 1900
Pictured next to Ivatt C1 Class Atlantic No. 990 *Henry Oakley* are an unidentified driver and fireman T. Stanley.

No. 990, *c.* 1898
GNR No. 990 was the prototype C1 Atlantic built at Doncaster Works in May 1898. The design for the locomotive originated from the need for greater power to haul the increasing size of trains at the time, which the Stirling Singles were struggling to do. A larger boiler was required and this necessitated employing a different wheel arrangement. H. A. Ivatt decided to adopt a 4-4-2 configuration from locomotives of a similar type finding success on the Philadelphia & Reading Railroad in the United States during this period. No. 990 was fitted with a 4-foot 8-inch boiler, had a firebox heating surface of 140.1 square feet, boiler pressure of 175 lb per square inch and tractive effort of 15,640 lb. No. 990 (named *Henry Oakley* in June 1900) had close to a forty-year career before it was withdrawn in October 1937 and subsequently went into preservation.

Foundry Overhead Crane, *c.* 1900

Built in 1881, Doncaster Works' Iron Foundry consisted of three bays; one large central bay with two smaller ones at either side. The first crane installed was manually operated from the foundry floor by ropes. In 1890 a steam-driven crane with 15-ton capacity was purchased from J. Booth & Bros of Rodley, Leeds. From the foundry many parts for steam locomotives were forged but with the introduction of diesel locomotives its importance dwindled. The shop's role was subsequently changed to accommodate crane and chain repairs.

Crimpsall Construction, 1900

During the 1890s Doncaster Works was becoming increasingly overwhelmed by the amount of work it was expected to carry out. To help alleviate the problem it was decided to extend the site to the Crimpsall Meadows, which were located next to the Works. The construction work started in 1899 by local firm H. Arnold & Son at a cost of £294,000. The Crimpsall Workshop was completed around 1901 and had space to repair approximately 100 locomotives. The photograph captures work progressing in June 1900.

Crimpsall Demolition, 2008

The Crimpsall Workshops were demolished in 2008. Photograph taken on 29 April 2008 and reproduced by courtesy of Derek Porter.

Stirling 2-2-2 No. 232, *c.* 1900
Although the Stirling Singles were normally fitted with 8-foot diameter driving wheels a number were produced with driving wheels of a smaller diameter. These variants included: 7-foot 1-inch, 7-foot 6-inch and 7-foot 7-inch wheels. No. 232 was one of two 7-foot 6-inch engines built in 1885 with a further twenty-one larger engines, with the same wheel size, built between 1886 and 1894. No. 232 is pictured around 1900, possibly at Doncaster Carr locomotive shed where it spent a large portion of its career. Withdrawal came in June 1906.

Tender Shop Construction, *c.* 1900

Completed around 1900, the Tender Repair Shop replaced an older shop located at the original Works site. The new shop was located on the west side of the Crimpsall Repair Shop and consisted of two large repair bays with a smaller machine bay. Space was provided in the two bays for the repair of thirty-two tenders. In the 1930s tender repair work was relocated to No. 1 bay of the Crimpsall Repair Shop and the Tender Shop became the Stripping Shop where locomotives were stripped of their parts and boiler and superheater repairs were carried out. Diesel locomotives were subsequently stripped in the building, which was demolished in 2008.

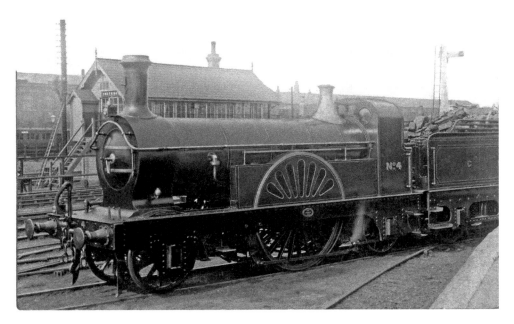

Stirling 2-2-2 No. 4, *c.* 1900

Pictured at Doncaster South signal box around 1900 is Stirling 2-2-2 Single No. 4, built at Doncaster Works in June 1868. It was one of twelve erected between 1868 and 1870 with 7-foot 1-inch driving wheels. The design for these locomotives originated with the Sturrock 229 Class, the main alterations being the substitution of some of the components for simpler alternatives to reduce costs. No. 4 was withdrawn while it was approaching forty years in service in June 1906. The last of these twelve engines left service in November 1907.

Ivatt Atlantic No. 251, *c.* 1902

No. 251 was built at Doncaster Works in December 1902 as a larger variation of the Ivatt C1 Atlantics and was the prototype engine for the following ninety-three locomotives of the class. The main difference over the smaller Atlantics was the large increase in the size of the boiler to 5 feet 6 inches, but the firebox also had a larger grate area and heating surface. No. 251 later had its original slide valves replaced by piston valves in December 1923. It also carried a Schmidt eighteen-element superheater and a Robinson thirty-two-element superheater from August 1918 and June 1932 respectively. Withdrawal for preservation came in July 1947.

Doncaster Works Crane, *c.* 1905

This locomotive started its life as Stirling-designed 0-4-4 engine No. 533 built at Doncaster in 1876 as part of the 120 Class. Leaving service in June 1905 it found a new lease of life as the Doncaster Works crane, its duties including handling materials and testing carriage brakes. It received a domed boiler in September 1925, but finally left service in November 1928 with a working life of fifty-two years.

Crimpsall – No. 418, 1909

Pictured awaiting attention at the Crimpsall shops on 1 July 1909 is No. 418. The locomotive is an Ivatt K1, later LNER Q1 Class engine and was built at Doncaster Works in January 1903 and its first allocation was to Colwick to haul coal traffic, which was its main task throughout its career. The class had a relatively short lifespan as all had left service by 1935; No. 418 (as LNER 3418) had been withdrawn in November 1929.

Above: **Ivatt Atlantic No. 1422,** *c.* 1908
At Doncaster station is Ivatt Large Atlantic No. 1422 posing for the camera along with an unidentified group of men. No. 1422 was built at Doncaster in 1908 and retained its slide valves until withdrawn in July 1945. The locomotive was noted as being allocated to Doncaster shed in 1912 and again on the eve of grouping.

Opposite page, bottom: **Doncaster Station**
Exterior view of Doncaster station in GNR days.

Crimpsall Locomotives Awaiting Repair, 1909

A scene outside the completed Crimpsall Repair Shop in mid-1909. The shop consisted of four large bays and two smaller bays with the locomotives seen here awaiting entry to one of the larger bays to receive repairs. A mixture of Ivatt and Stirling engines can be seen and they comprise: Ivatt Single (unidentified), Ivatt 4-4-0 No. 1327, Stirling 0-4-4 well tank No. 159, Ivatt 0-6-0ST Nos 1259 and 1262 and the front end of an unidentified Ivatt 2-8-0.

Crimpsall South Side No. 867, 1923

Pictured at the south side of the Crimpsall Repair Shop in June 1923 are two withdrawn 2-4-0 6-foot 6-inch passenger locomotives designed by Patrick Stirling. On the right is No. 867 but the number of the locomotive on the left is unidentifiable. No. 867 was one of 139 engines built to Stirling's design between 1867 and 1895. The locomotives were built at Avonside Engine Co., Yorkshire Engine Co., Doncaster Works and Kitson and Co. No. 867 was built at Doncaster Works in June 1892 in the 206 series but was later modified by H. A. Ivatt to include a 4-foot 5-inch-diameter boiler and flat-topped cab.

Crimpsall Interior, *c.* 1909

This view of the Crimpsall Repair Shop shows one of the two smaller bays that were found between the end and middle bays of the building. Measuring 520 feet long and 30 feet wide, the two small bays housed machine fitters, coppersmiths and boilersmiths who worked on parts from the locomotives in for repair. The man in the foreground wearing the bowler hat is a foreman.

Fitters, *c.* 1910
This formal group photograph shows the fitters that were employed at Doncaster Works.

GNR Brass Finishers, *c.* 1910
The Doncaster Works brass finishers pose for the camera.

Doncaster Railway Station, *c.* 1910

A scene at Doncaster railway station showing a number of locomotives including a couple of Ivatt 4-4-0s and possibly an Ivatt 0-6-0ST. A temporary station was first opened by the GNR at Doncaster during September 1848 and located to the south of the present site of the station. A permanent station was opened in September 1850 and remodelled in 1938.

C1 Large Boiler Atlantic No. 1460, *c.* 1910

The driver and fireman pose in front of one of Ivatt's large boiler C1 Class Atlantics. No. 1460 was the penultimate example of the class to be completed during November 1910. It was built with Schmidt-type superheater and piston valves when new. The superheater was later altered to the Robinson-type with twenty-four elements in May 1917. It was again updated when a Robinson thirty-two element superheater was fitted in June 1931. Only the final ten engines were fitted with Schmidt superheaters when built and their use was later discontinued by Gresley in 1914 in favour of the Robinson-type. October 1945 saw the withdrawal of No. 1460 as LNER No. 4460.

Frame and Motion, 1911
Taken in February 1911 the photograph shows the frame and inside motion for a GNR 0-6-0. The frame was that of an old engine and had been prepared at the Works for the purpose of demonstration and instruction.

Superheated D1 No. 51, 1911

Pictured on 4 March 1911 is a broadside of the first of Ivatt's Superheated D1 Class 4-4-0 locomotives – No. 51. It was built at Doncaster Works in March 1911. Fifteen were erected with superheaters and were similar in design to the members of the D1 Class with saturated boilers. Alterations included larger cylinders, piston valves, longer smokebox, repositioned bogie and an increased boiler pitch. The superheater was the Schmidt-type with eighteen elements. No. 51 was a long-time Leeds resident working local passenger services with an occasional run to London. Allocations to Scotland and Norwich came after grouping when new classes superseded the D1s and their usefulness declined. No. 51 left service in February 1946 and the class was extinct by the end of 1950.

J22 Superheated No. 554

Before his retirement, H. A. Ivatt produced a design for an 0-6-0 locomotive capable of hauling heavy goods trains that could also be used for passenger services. The first locomotive for this purpose was completed in 1908 and classified J21. At the same time experiments were taking place with superheated boilers and by 1911 it had been decided to fit superheaters to the 0-6-0s. Fifteen were built in 1911 to Ivatt's specifications and classified J22, later sub-classified as the 521 series. A further ninety-five were built to the modified design by Gresley before grouping and sub-classified as the 536 series. No. 554 was built at Doncaster in June 1913 and is pictured there on 13th to illustrate the use of Gresley's single anti-vacuum valve. All earlier engines were later fitted with this type replacing twin anti-vacuum valves. Withdrawal came in June 1962 as BR No. 64203.

Opposite page: C1 'Klondyke' Atlantic No. 252

This locomotive was the first of the final batch of C1 'Klondyke' Atlantics to be built. Construction took place at Doncaster Works, No. 252 being built in May and the last, No. 258, being completed in June 1903. No. 252 is photographed at Doncaster at the end of January 1913 with an extended smokebox. After a failed experiment with 'Notter's Patent' spark arrester, the smokebox was extended by 1 foot 2¾ inches to create extra space that acted as a spark arrester. The majority of the 'Klondyke' Atlantics were altered to accommodate this feature before grouping. No. 252 was a long-time resident in London before the formation of the LNER, later moving to Cambridge and finally Retford, where it was withdrawn in July 1945. It was the last of the class to leave service.

Upper Turnery, *c.* 1916
The Upper Turnery was located in the long building facing Doncaster station, which dates from the early 1850s and also housed the Lower Turnery, Carriage Trimming Shop and later the Central Drawing Office. This scene captured from the marking-off table in July 1916 shows women at work in the Upper Turnery manufacturing various components. The building later became offices and in the 1980s was awarded Grade II listed status.

Gresley H3 No. 1640

The GNR H2 and H3 classes of 2-6-0 locomotives appeared as the result of a lack of dedicated express goods engines working for the GNR during the early years of the twentieth century. Before their introduction a lot of passenger engines had to be used for goods services and they were unsuitable for this task. The first of the new engines to enter service was No. 1630 in August 1912, classified H2. A further nine were built before a larger boiler version was introduced in April 1914 with No. 1640 seen here. The diameter of the boiler was increased by 10 inches to 5 feet 6 inches, which allowed a Robinson-type twenty-four-element superheater to be fitted. The H2 and H3 classes became LNER K1 and K2 classes at grouping and all were in service at nationalisation. No. 1640 left service as BR No. 61730 in August 1957.

No. 404, 1917

This Ivatt K1 0-8-0 locomotive was built at Doncaster in May 1902, but is pictured at the Works in June 1917 after it was fitted with a Willans feed water heater, visible between the second and third wheels. No. 404 was built with a saturated boiler but this was later changed to include a Robinson-type superheater in October 1914. The Willans heater caused the number of superheater elements to be reduced to sixteen and later fourteen when the system was modified in 1920. The history of the Willans apparatus on this engine is unclear and it is unknown if it was removed before the locomotive was withdrawn in April 1929. In March 1925 the locomotive had been renumbered 3404 and reclassified Q1 by the LNER.

Gresley Class J23 No. 215

This 0-6-0T locomotive, No. 215, was built at Doncaster Works in July 1919 as part of the 168 Series of Gresley's Class J23. The class had originated in 1913, specifically designed to work on the tracks of the West Riding of Yorkshire. As part of the 168 series, the locomotive was slightly modified from the first ten engines built. The water capacity of the side tanks was increased by 20 gallons, the layout of the bunker was changed to create space for more coal and the cab also saw minor alterations. Forty of the class were produced before grouping, in three series, and all survived to be withdrawn by BR between May 1959 and September 1963.

Gresley N2 0-6-2T No. 1608, 1921

No. 1608 was built at Doncaster in May 1921, one of ten erected there between December 1920 and August 1921. Fifty were built concurrently by the North British Locomotive Co., who completed the order in April 1921. The N2 Class, to which these 0-6-2T engines belonged, was based on the N1 Class designed by Ivatt, but modified and improved by Gresley. The changes included superheating the boiler, increasing the water capacity by 400 gallons to 2,000 gallons and employing piston valves with larger cylinders increased in size by an inch to 19 inches by 26 inches. The class were employed specifically on London suburban services, with the condensing apparatus seen here fitted for this purpose. No. 1608 was withdrawn from King's Cross shed in November 1959.

Gresley A1 No. 1470, 1922

Gresley A1 Class Pacific No. 1470 *Great Northern* poses for an official photograph on 23 May 1922. The A1 Pacifics had a 6-foot 5-inch diameter boiler, firebox heating surface of 215 square feet, boiler pressure of 180 lb per square inch and tractive effort of 29,835 lb placing them well in front of the Ivatt Atlantics and meaning they were very capable of hauling the heaviest trains of the day. For these new Pacifics a suitable design of tender was required after the intention of using Atlantic-type tenders was deemed unsuitable. The new eight-wheel tenders had a capacity of 5,000 gallons of water and 8 tons of coal.

First Gresley Pacific Frames, 1921

Pictured in the last few months of 1921 are the frames for the first Gresley Pacific. They were laid at Doncaster at the end of August 1921 and construction work was completed by March the following year, taking about eight months from start to finish. The main frames were made from steel plate 1⅛ inches deep, 4 feet 1½ inches apart at the front closing to 3 feet 5 inches at the rear. Extra support was provided for the firebox in the form of additional frames bolted to the rear end, 6 feet ½ inch apart and an inch deep.

No. 1470 in Works

At the time this picture was taken, 24 March 1922, Gresley's pioneer A1 Pacific was nearing its entry to traffic and is seen being lifted off the pit in the new erecting shop at Doncaster Works. The Gresley Pacific was a response to the growing demands that were being put on the locomotives in service at the time just as Ivatt's Atlantic design was previously. Another similarity is that the design was inspired by another American locomotive, the Pennsylvanian Railroad's K4 Pacific. No. 1470 *Great Northern* entered traffic on 11 April 1922 with the second, No. 1471, following in July. Only two were built before grouping but prior to that the GNR ordered a further ten engines.

Gresley H4 No. 1000 Cab Interior, 1922
A view inside the cab of H4 Class No. 1000.

Gresley H4 No. 1000, 1921
In 1920/21 ten H4 Class engines were built at Doncaster Works to Gresley's design. These locomotives were similar to the H3 Class locomotives but they had a few differences. The main one was the addition of a third cylinder, which came after this arrangement found success on Gresley's 2-8-0 O2 Class locomotives. The size of the boiler was increased to a diameter of 6 feet, the number of superheater elements was increased to thirty-two and the pressure was raised to 180 lb per square inch. The locomotives became LNER Class K3 at grouping and Gresley later used the design as standard but made modifications over the years with 183 examples of post-grouping engines existing by 1937. No. 1000 was withdrawn in July 1962.

4
Doncaster's Great Northern Railway Wagon Works

GNR Wagon Works Wheelwrights, 1914
A formal group photograph of the wheelwrights employed at Doncaster Carr Wagon Works in 1914 is seen here. These men would have been very busy as the Works built and repaired a large variety of wagons, including open wagons, goods brakes, horseboxes, gas tanks, fish vans and breakdown cranes. In 1923 reorganisation occurred and only repairs and reconditioning were carried out.

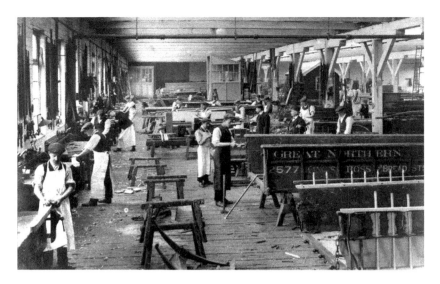

Dray Shop, 1914

The dray shop is pictured in 1914 with employees hard at work. The area was located in the south shop at the Carr Wagon Works where the GNR's vans and road vehicles were also built. The south shop was also used for wagon repairs for which ten of the fifteen roads were allocated and in total it could hold approximately 220 vehicles. The north shop was the other main building on the site and it facilitated new wagon construction. Comprising seven roads, the shop had space available for approximately 140 wagons.

Wagon Works Yard, 1919

Wagon work was transferred from Doncaster Works in 1889 as space was running out at the main site. New buildings were constructed at the Carr, which was located 2 miles south of Doncaster. The new site was also advantageous because it was located near wagon marshalling yards, which could help to handle the large amount of wagon traffic at the Works. This view of the Works yard was taken at the end of 1919 and shows the large amount of timber in stock for use in wagon construction and repair. The Wagon Works returned to Doncaster Works in the mid-1960s.

5
London & North Eastern Railway Carriages

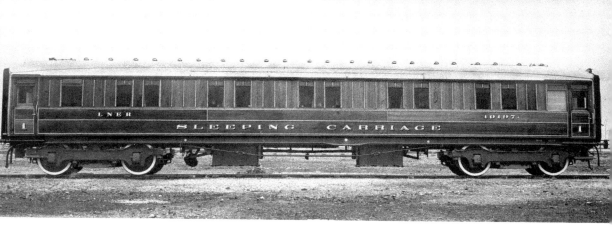

Sleeping Carriage No. 10197

No. 10197 (later renumbered 1237) was built in 1924 as a first-class sleeping carriage to diagram 17 design. Four vehicles were built to the design in 1924 with further examples being built up until 1927. Each carriage was 61 feet 9 inches long and 9 feet wide with ten compartments for ten passengers. Some of the carriages built to the design were later fitted with two-tier berths in the compartments at either end of the carriage. Each compartment was separated by a door which could be unlocked and opened to make the compartment a double. For the exterior teak panels were used, while the interior was plainly decorated in white with polished woodwork.

Above: **Triplet Restaurant Car,** *c.* **1929**
Pictured around 1929 is the triplet restaurant-first/kitchen/restaurant-third built for the London–Edinburgh non-stop 'Flying Scotsman' service that started in May 1928. The Flying Scotsman train also included a third brake, third composite, first, hair dressing/ladies room third, two thirds and a bogie brake. The new triplet restaurant car received special attention in its interior design with Allom & Co. being employed for the decoration, which was described as Louis XIV in style. Paintwork was stone-coloured with blue and green highlights applied to mouldings in first and third class respectively. A similar colour scheme was used in other aspects of the furnishing.

Opposite page, bottom: **Carriage Trimming Shop**
The Carriage Trimming Shop was built in 1866 to the north of the turneries building (later Denison House). Workers are pictured hard at work on various upholstering tasks in May 1930. During the latter year Doncaster built approximately fifty-five new carriages as part of the 1930/31 Carriage Building Programme. 280 had been ordered from various Works to replace 369 old vehicles. At the end of the year, 180 still had not been built as well as three from the 1929 order and these were incorporated into the one for 1931/2. The Carriage Trimming Shop became the Chief Mechanical Engineer's office during the Second World War after it moved from King's Cross.

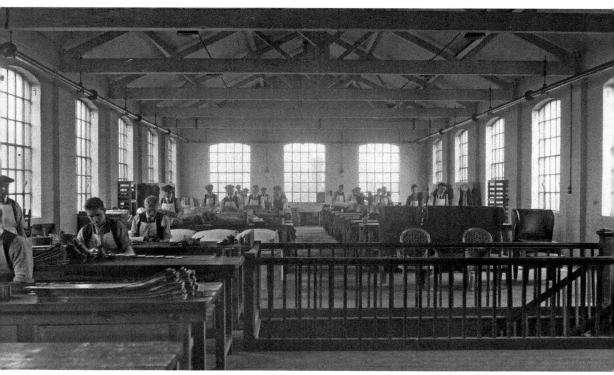

Silver Jubilee Carriages Nos 1581–2, 1935

The 'Silver Jubilee' service appeared in 1935 running return journeys between Newcastle and King's Cross and was aimed at businessmen. The new service required a dedicated set of locomotives and stock; the result being the A4 Class Pacifics and this new, specially designed coaching stock. Articulated carriages were used (as illustrated here) for the seven which were constructed at Doncaster Works. They included twin open-brake/semi-open first (Nos 1581–2 pictured here), triplet first-class/kitchen car/third-class, third-class/brake-third carriages. The open brake had five compartments seating thirty, while the semi-open first had three compartments with a smoking saloon fitted with large armchairs, which also seated thirty. The total capacity of the train was 233 passengers.

Chief Engineer's Saloon No. 900580, 1936

This carriage was built at Doncaster in 1936 for use by the Chief Engineer. It was 60 feet 1½ inches long, 9 feet 3 inches wide and steel panelled with an open balcony, saloon, toilet, guards' compartment, bathroom and galley, which were connected by a side corridor. When in service the carriage was based at Stratford before spending time in Scotland prior to leaving service in the early 1980s to work preservation lines.

Coronation Set Interior, 1937

A view of the interior of the twin first-class carriage of the 1937 LNER Coronation service carriage set. The original intention was for the set to follow the general layout of the preceding Silver Jubilee special service set that appeared in 1935, i.e. a compartment and corridor layout. However, it was decided that this new set should be built with an open layout. Objections were raised to this decision and to appease protestors, partitions were included in the design and every set of seats in first class and every second set in third class were partitioned. The job of designing the interior was trusted to Acton Surgey Ltd who employed an Art Deco style for various features of the decoration. Rexine (imitation leather) was used for surfaces, and anodised aluminium fret with aluminium architraves were specifically used in first class as were swivelling armchairs, which were luxuriously upholstered. The general colour used in both first and third class was green.

Above: **Coronation Set Exterior, 1937**

The Coronation coach set was brought into service after the success of the Silver Jubilee service and its dedicated set of carriages. Three new sets of coaches were built at Doncaster in 1937 – two for the Coronation service and a spare set, which could be used on any of the named services but was identical to the Coronation set. A total of twenty-six carriages were constructed. The two Coronation sets had nine coaches, while the spare set had eight coaches; the extra carriage on the Coronation service was the beaver-tail observation car. The Coronation set received its name to celebrate the Coronation of King George VI. The coaches were built with teak-framed bodies with panels made from steel. The carriage bodies were 56 feet 2½ inches long and 9 feet 2¼ inches wide; they were articulated making four sets of two carriages. They comprised third-brake/third, kitchen-third/third, kitchen-third/third-brake, first/first and the observation car. This latter was slightly shorter than the other carriages at 51 feet 9 inches long and 9 feet 2¼ inches wide.

Opposite page, bottom: **Coronation Set, 1937**

Pictured at Retford behind LNER No. 4489 *Dominion of Canada* in July 1937 is the front of the Coronation set. The livery first applied to the Coronation carriages was two shades of blue – Marlborough blue and garter blue – which were chosen from colours sponsored by the British Colour Council as part of the celebrations for the Coronation of King George VI. The bottom half of the carriages – wheels, bogies, etc. – were painted black, while the roofs were painted in an aluminium finish. The body was trimmed in stainless steel with the service name and carriage numbers also being applied in stainless steel. The bottom of the side skirts on the locomotive and tender sheets are also fitted with stainless steel strips for the service. Five A4s were modified in this manner for the Coronation service.

West Riding Set Semi-Open First

The West Riding Ltd set was the last of the three streamlined sets produced by the LNER. The first service commenced on 27 September 1937, leaving the capital destined for Leeds and then Bradford. The set comprised twin open-third-brake/kitchen-open-third, twin open firsts, twin open-third/kitchen-open-third and twin open-third/open-third-brake. The exterior appearance of the set was the same as the Coronation carriages, with only the name different, while the interior was also similar but the colour scheme was altered. As with the other streamlined sets it was stored during the Second World War, finding a place at Copley Hill. It returned to service in May 1949, but in 1950 the twin open firsts were destroyed by fire.

Cleaning, 1944

Two women are cleaning an unidentified carriage in March 1944. As during the First World War, Doncaster Works was heavily involved with the manufacture of materials for the war effort.

American GIs, 1943

During the Christmas period of 1943 American GIs celebrate with Doncaster Works staff. The picture was taken in the cleared site of the Main Carriage Shop, which was destroyed by fire in December 1940.

American Soldiers, 1944
Photographed at Doncaster Works in June 1944 is a group of American soldiers with carriage and wagon works managerial staff. The group is pictured in front of Ambulance Train Boiler Car No. 4301.

Third-Class Prototype No. 1347

During the latter stages of the Second World War, the LNER board began to look at its current coaching stock and how it would fare in the post-war period. In 1944 it was estimated that 2,500 vehicles were due for withdrawal and that 4,500 new vehicles were required. These figures were later increased to 5,500 vehicles to be withdrawn and built. The new vehicles were to take on a certain degree of standardisation, which included the use of all-steel bodies and a break in general with existing carriage-construction practice. No. 1347 was one of two prototype carriages built at Doncaster in 1945 (the other was No. 1531) for third- and first-class carriages respectively. They were built with steel side sheets, teak frames and a new style of windows. Another new feature was a change to the internal layout, which now included transverse vestibules to ease passenger congestion when boarding and alighting the carriage.

Third-Class Prototype No. 1347 Interior, 1945

Also pictured here is the interior of carriage No. 1347. Built to diagram 329 design the carriage had seven compartments that provided seating for forty-two passengers in a body which measured 63 feet by 9 feet 3 inches. The interior of the new LNER stock was criticised for being too old-fashioned and of a poor standard in relation to its contemporaries produced by the Great Western Railway and Southern Railway. Both pictures were taken in May 1945.

Carriage Drawing Office Staff, 1945
Members of the Carriage Drawing Office staff pose for a group photograph on 11 May 1945.

Rebuilding Carriage Shops
Preparing the site for rebuilding the Carriage Shops, April 1947, after the fire of December 1940. The main carriage building shop was destroyed in the fire and also caused an estimated £18,000 worth of damage to existing coaching stock. The replacement building was completed in 1948.

6
Doncaster Carr Locomotive Depot

Doncaster Carr Loco Shed Mechanical Coaler

The original engine shed was located at Doncaster station and had space for thirty locomotives. The allocation to Doncaster far exceeded this capacity and by the mid- to late 1860s more space was sought and found about a mile south of Doncaster station. Work started in May 1874 but it was not until March 1876 that the shed was finally opened. The cost of the works totalled £37,000 and the building had twelve roads with space for 100 engines, measuring 420 feet by 180 feet. The mechanical coaling Plant was installed at Doncaster Carr in the late 1920s and had a capacity of 500 tons, being similar in design to those found at King's Cross, Peterborough and York. It underwent a heavy overhaul during 1954 and survived a further twelve years or so until removed when the shed was converted for use by diesels. Taking on coal from the mechanical coaler is Gresley A1 No. 2543 *Melton*.

Doncaster Carr Loco Shed, *c.* 1939

A view of the north end of Doncaster Carr locomotive shed *c.* 1939, looking towards Doncaster. Visible to the right is the north coal stage. When the shed was opened in 1876, two coal stages were provided at either end of the shed yard. The north stage was rebuilt in 1898 to provide a space underneath the stage for the drivers and to improve productivity. When the mechanical coaler was installed around 1926 (where this view is probably taken from) the north stage was retained while the southern one was demolished.

Doncaster Carr Loco Shed A1 Class No. 2555, Late 1920s

Built in February 1925, No. 2555 *Centenary* is pictured at Doncaster Carr locomotive shed, possibly during one of its allocations or after a works visit. The date of the picture is unknown but it is probably late 1920s to early 1930s before application of the locomotive number on the side of the cab became standard. The locomotive had ten visits to Doncaster Works before its first heavy repair started in October 1932. It also had a lengthy allocation to Doncaster shed during this period: February 1925 to December 1935, broken only by a few weeks at Grantham in October 1929.

7
London & North Eastern Railway Locomotives

Gresley Class O2/2 No. 487N, 1923

Gresley Class O2/2 2-8-0 locomotive No. 487N was built at Doncaster Works in October 1923 and is pictured there after completion. It was placed into the second part of the class with fourteen others as they were built to conform to the new LNER load gauge, which required certain features being lowered. No. 487N is actually fitted with a larger chimney in this picture, however it was replaced with a shorter one at a later date. These LNER engines also differed from those built by the GNR as their crank axles were manufactured from separate components whereas the GNR ones had them made from one piece. In October 1944 this engine was fitted with a side-window cab, which did not follow with a number of locomotives built like No. 487N. The last alteration occurred in July 1958.

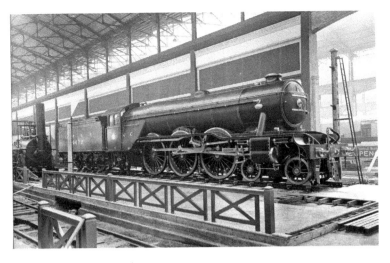

Wembley Exhibition *Flying Scotsman*, 1924

The British Empire Exhibition was held at Wembley in 1924 and 1925. For the 1924 exhibition No. 4472 *Flying Scotsman*, along with Stockton & Darlington Railway No. 1 *Locomotion* (seen on the left) were chosen to represent the LNER in the Palace of Engineering. A railway line was specifically built for the exhibition, linking the site with Marylebone station. The photograph was taken during March 1924.

P1 No. 2394 Frames, 1924/1925

Pictured in the Doncaster Works' New Erecting Shop are the frames for P1 Class 2-8-2 locomotive No. 2394. In the background production can be seen to be progressing on the first P1 No. 2393. The frames were made from two 1⅛-inch-wide steel plates that were 4 feet 1½ inches apart. At the rear the spacing was reduced to 3 feet 5 inches and additional frames were added here to support the firebox and were 6 feet ½ inch apart. The engine was completed in November 1925.

A1 No. 2543, c. 1924

An impressive sight would have been on offer if the occupants of the houses in the background looked out of their window on this particular day, as Gresley A1 No. 2543 is pictured waiting near Balby Bridge, Doncaster. The locomotive was built in June 1924 and is pictured before 1925/1926 when the unnamed members of the class began to receive names. The majority took the names of racehorses with No. 2543 acquiring *Melton*, which won the Derby and St. Leger of 1885. The locomotive was rebuilt as A3 in September 1947 and withdrawn in June 1963.

J72 No. 500, 1925

LNER Class J72 0-6-0T locomotive, No. 500, was the first of a batch of ten engines to be built at Doncaster Works in 1925. The class had originated with the NER as Class E1 designed by Raven. Seventy-five had been built at Darlington and Armstrong, Whitworth & Co. before grouping, with a further twenty-eight built after nationalisation for BR at Darlington. The construction of the ten at Doncaster can be said to be a somewhat strange decision as they followed a pattern which was alien to those followed by Doncaster Works including Darlington-type smokebox door and NER buffers. No. 500 was withdrawn in September 1961.

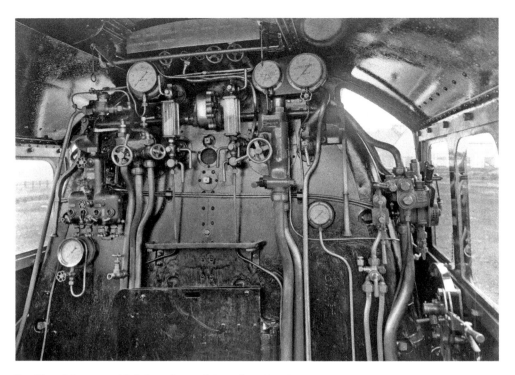

P1 Class No. 2393 (Cab Interior and Exterior Views), 1925

The idea of producing a powerful 2-8-2 goods engine based on the O2 Class but with an A1 Class boiler was first put forward by Gresley in 1922 and the design work started in mid-1923. The intention for this type of locomotive was for it to haul extremely heavy coal trains into the London area. Two engines, Nos 2393 and 2394, were completed in June and November 1925 and classified P1. The cost of constructing the engines was close to £21,000, which was £4,000 over the original estimated price for both. In service the engines proved more than capable of hauling the heavy loads expected of them. However, the capacity of the track proved to be their downfall as it was not big enough to accommodate the 100 or more wagons they could pull, and a lot of stopping and starting was involved so that other trains could pass it. Thompson withdrew both locomotives in July 1945 and they were subsequently scrapped. Also pictured is the cab of No. 2393, which was based on the design for the A1 Class Pacific engines.

N2 No. 897, 1925

Class N2/3 0-6-2T locomotive No. 897 was built at Doncaster Works in December 1925 to Gresley's designs. The class had originated, under the same classification, during 1920 as an improved version of the Ivatt N1 Class. Sixty were built before grouping for the GNR with a further forty-seven built by the LNER. Only six were built at Doncaster; No. 897 was the last of the order to be completed, with the others built for the LNER by Beyer, Peacock & Co., Hawthorn, Leslie & Co. and the Yorkshire Engine Co. In 1946 the locomotive was renumbered 9567 before becoming BR No. 69567 in July 1948. It lost its Westinghouse brake equipment in December 1938 when it was fitted with vacuum brakes. Withdrawal came in April 1959.

Directors and Engineers at Eden Grove, Late 1920s

At Eden Grove sports club in Doncaster are a number of important people involved with the LNER. The photograph was taken in the late 1920s. Back row: R. A. Thom, A. H. Peppercorn, Colonel Firth, -?-. Front row (left to right): Nigel Gresley, Sir William Whitelaw, -?-, Sir Ralph Wedgwood.

First Gresley A3 No. 2743, 1928

The number of Gresley A1 Class had reached fifty-two by 1925, with thirty-two built at Doncaster. They were proving themselves capable engines but were experiencing some teething problems. By 1928 some of these had been addressed but it was found that the locomotives could be improved further. A new higher-pressure boiler set at 220 lb per square inch with a larger forty-element superheater and cylinders with a diameter of 19 inches were fitted first to a number of A1s for trial. After the success of these the construction of ten new engines classified A3 was authorised in 1927. The first of the new A3s to appear was No. 2743 *Felstead* in August 1928 and it is seen here with a corridor tender. Twenty-six more A3s were built, the last one entering service in 1935.

Corridor Tender Frames, 1928

A corridor tender is pictured under construction at Doncaster Works on 10 May 1928. This new type of tender was introduced for the non-stop services as it was necessary for two sets of crews to be employed on the journey. The footplate was connected to the first carriage of the train by a corridor 5 feet high and 18 inches wide in the tender so the crew could be changed during the journey and rest in the carriage. During 1928 ten tenders of this new type were built and fitted to the new A3 Class and A1 Class engines. Coal capacity was increased by 1 ton over the GN-type tenders to 9 tons with both being able to carry the same capacity of water, 5,000 gallons. These corridor tenders later found employment behind the A4 Class locomotives.

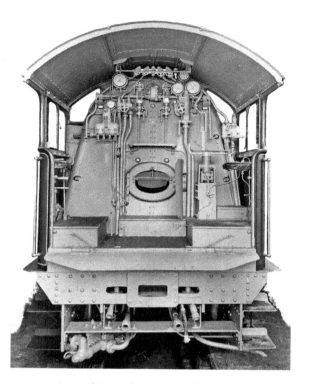

A1 and A3 Cabs, 1924 and 1928

Two views of the cabs fitted to the A1 and A3 Class Pacific locomotives. The A1 Cab (left) belongs to No. 2544 *Lemberg* and the picture was taken on 15 July 1924. The A3 cab belongs to an unidentified locomotive but the picture was taken on 27 November 1928, suggesting that it was one of the first ten A3s to be built and backed up by the fact it is left-hand drive. The cabs were reduced in size on the engines built after 1924 to comply with stricter loading gauges than on the GN section, with earlier engines altered. The seats on both are backless and this feature was not introduced until 1935.

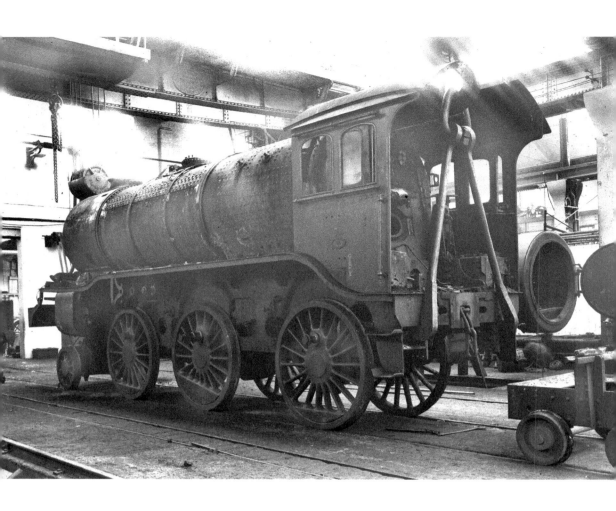

Above: **J52 No. 3971, 1929**

No. 3971 was the first of ten Stirling 0-6-0ST engines built at Doncaster between August 1894 and October 1895 as part of GNR Class J14. Twenty had been produced at the Works previously, as construction of the class had begun in December 1892. A further twenty were built by Neilson & Co. before the final two were built at Doncaster in 1897. At grouping the majority of locomotives were classified J53 by the LNER. After Stirling's death in 1895 Ivatt took over and produced eighty-five similar 0-6-0STs but with a 4-foot 5-inch boiler with a dome. These engines were classified J13 by the GNR and J52 by the LNER. Three J14s had been fitted with the J13 boiler before grouping and the LNER continued these modifications after grouping. No. 3971 was altered in November 1928 and reclassified J52. Some of the J14s were fitted with condensing equipment to operate on the Metropolitan widened lines when built and No. 3971 was one of them. The engine was pictured in London between February and April 1929 for the chief mechanical engineer's record book. It was withdrawn in April 1953.

Opposite page, top: **K3 No. 188, 1930**

K3 Class 2-6-0 No. 188 is pictured being lifted off its wheels in the Crimpsall Repair Shop during July 1930. The engine was built in March 1925 as part of the sixty-strong 17 series that were all constructed at Darlington, forming class part two. As they were built at Darlington these locomotives included some NER-style features such as the chimney and the cab. Repairs of the class were usually dealt with by the Works responsible for the area the locomotive was allocated to at the time. This usually meant visiting either Doncaster, Darlington or Cowlairs. From the mid-1930s the class began to be solely maintained by Doncaster. No. 188 as BR No. 61856 was withdrawn from Ardsley in December 1962.

Opposite page, bottom: **K3 No. 1300, 1929**

In 1929 twenty K3s were built at Doncaster Works with a change of features from earlier engines, which saw them form class part three. In April 1929 No. 1330 was the first to be built with Westinghouse brakes and vacuum ejector (removed from all in the early 1930s), left-hand drive, screw reversing gear, long-lap valve gear and straight-sided tenders. All of these engines entered service to the north-east area and were allocated to York, Heaton and Tweedmouth forcing B16s at these sheds to be moved on. No. 1300 was renumbered 61870 by BR and was withdrawn in July 1962.

No. 2548 in Crimpsall, 1930

At the start of July 1930 Gresley A1 Pacific No. 2548, *Galtee More*, was coming to the end of a general repair and is shown here in the process of being lifted back on to its wheels in the Crimpsall Repair Shop. The repairs had started on 20 May and the locomotive left the shops on 5 July after it received a change of boiler. It replaced the one originally fitted and the replacement came from No. 2557, *Blair Athol*. No. 2548 was built at Doncaster in September 1924, rebuilt to the A3 Class in October 1945 and left service as BR No. 60049 in December 1962.

A3 No. 2596, 1930

On 5 March 1930 Gresley Class A3 4-6-2 locomotive No. 2596, *Manna*, posed for its official picture after being built at Doncaster Works in February of that year. The name of the locomotive had originally appeared with Gresley A1 No. 2553 when it was built in December 1924. However, No. 2553 was renamed *Prince of Wales* in November 1926 as it was the locomotive seen by the Prince of Wales (later King Edward VIII) on a visit to Doncaster Works. Only one other name change occurred involving an A1 engine when No. 2563, *William Whitelaw*, became *Tagalie* in July 1941. The former was to be used on an A4 engine. As with BR No. 60085, *Manna* was withdrawn in October 1964.

J50 No. 2789, *c.* 1930

The GNR J23 0-6-0T Class, designed by Gresley, contained two variations of engines: one with a 4-foot 2-inch boiler and the other with a 4-foot 5-inch boiler and they were later classified J51 and J50 respectively by the LNER. After grouping, the J50 design was chosen to be group standard and a total of seventy-two were built at Doncaster Works and Gorton Works between 1924 and 1939. No. 2789 was built in March 1930, the first of the final six to be built at Doncaster. It was part of the 583 series (J50/3) and thirty-two engines of this series had been built at the Works previously between 1926 and 1927. A number of improvements over the GNR engines were incorporated in the design for the new J50s, which included steam brakes, improved cab ventilators, balanced wheels and larger axle journals. Fourteen more engines were built at Gorton Works between 1938 and 1939 in the 599 series (J50/4).

O2 Class No. 2954, 1932

No. 2954 was the first O2 Class 2-8-0 locomotive to be built after a gap in construction of eight years. Fifty were to be ordered in 1923 but ex-railway operating division 2-8-0 engines were bought instead becoming LNER O4 Class locomotives, which negated the need to build any O2 Class engines. Fifteen were scheduled to be built in 1930 but the first, No. 2954, did not appear until April 1932. This and other locomotives built afterwards were classified O2/3 as they had side-window cabs, second-hand group-standard 4,200-gallon tenders and steam brakes and they conformed to the 13-foot loading gauge of the G.E. section. The locomotive was withdrawn as BR No. 63947 in April 1961.

A3 No. 2751, 1933

Class A3 4-6-2 locomotive No. 2751, *Humorist*, was built at Doncaster Works in April 1929. In the early 1930s it became Doncaster Works' resident 'guinea pig' in trials with different types of smoke-lifting features. These experiments arose as the result of an accident, involving an LMS locomotive, that was caused by smoke being blown in the direction of the cab blocking the view of the driver and fireman. Four arrangements (some included alterations while on trial) were fitted to the locomotive between 1931 and 1933. *Humorist* is pictured in April 1933 after the fourth trial had taken place in March. This involved cutting the top of the smokebox at an angle of 22 degrees to force air around the chimney with wind vanes fitted at either side to aid this idea. The arrangement was slightly successful but problematic eddy currents were still present at the rear of the chimney and extra vanes were fitted there to stop this, which the photograph has been taken to depict. After a further trial this was found successful but needed the addition of larger vanes, which was found to be a satisfactory solution to the problem. However, despite these trials no other locomotives were changed and No. 2751 regained its original appearance in January 1934. *Humorist* was again involved in trials in 1937 when fitted with a Kylchap double blastpipe and chimney.

Doncaster Works Old Weigh House, 1933

This picture, taken at the end of September 1933, depicts the old Weigh House at Doncaster Works, which was built in 1893 and located near to Doncaster station. By the time of the picture it was becoming increasingly outdated and as a result a new weigh house was built between the Crimpsall Repair Shop and the paint shop in 1935. The new building was installed with 'Voiron' weighing equipment.

V1 Construction, 1933

This scene captured in August 1933 shows the cutting of the frames with an acetylene cutter for a V1 Class 2-6-2T locomotive. The first of the class emerged from Doncaster Works in September 1930. Twenty-eight were built in the initial order, all at Doncaster, which was the only Works that produced the class. Eighty-two in total had been built by 1939 at which time alterations were made to the boiler and these new engines were classified V3. Subsequently, the boilers of the V1 Class were changed to those of the new class and they were consequently reclassified V3.

P2 No. 2001, 1934

By the early 1930s the Edinburgh–Aberdeen route was proving problematic as loads were increasing and the engines available were not up to the challenges presented. Gresley specifically designed a locomotive for this task, employing a 2-8-2 wheel configuration for improved tractive effort and better adhesion. After initial deliberation over the design and features to be used on the new locomotive the drawing for what would be the first, No. 2001 *Cock O' The North*, appeared in March 1934 and the engine was completed in May 1934. It was fitted with Lentz rotary cam poppet valve gear, Kylchap double blastpipe and chimney, A.C.F.I. feed water heater and large smoke deflectors. Five more locomotives were ordered but they differed in some way from the original engine. No. 2002 *Earl Marischal* had conventional valves and motion, No. 2005 *Thane of Fife* had a normal chimney layout and No. 2006 *Wolf of Badenoch* had a modified firebox. The last four were also streamlined when built.

A3 No. 2500, 1934

The last A3 Class engines were ordered from Doncaster Works towards the end of 1933 and numbered nine in total. To speed up construction Gorton Works was employed to make components so they could be assembled at Doncaster. The frames for the first, No. 2500 *Windsor Lad,* were laid in February 1934 and it is pictured here in June 1934 completed. These new engines included features such as perforated steam collectors housed in the 'banjo'-shaped dome at the top of the boiler. They were also fitted with 'sine wave' superheater elements, which were used on the early P2 Class engines. However, they were found to be unsuitable due to erosion problems and were promptly removed. *Windsor Lad* was among the early withdrawals of the class, leaving service in September 1961.

P2 No. 2002, 1934

No. 2002 *Earl Marischal* was the second P2 Class 2-8-2 locomotive to appear but it did not follow exactly the specifications of the first of the class, No. 2001 *Cock O' The North.* No. 2002 was built in October 1934 with Walschaerts/Gresley valve gear with 9-inch piston valves. The use of piston valves caused a couple of problems during the first months of service. On a number of occasions it had trouble maintaining good boiler pressure and this necessitated changing the diameter of the blastpipe top to 5¾ inches with No. 3 taper blocks, which sufficiently improved the boiler pressure. Further, the engine had trouble adequately lifting smoke when at short cut-off hindering the view of the driver and this was attributed to the piston valves. As a result extra smoke-lifting plates were fitted improving dispersal but causing the nameplate to be positioned 7¼ inches lower than they are pictured here. *Earl Marischal* was rebuilt by Thompson in June 1944.

First A4 No. 2509, 1935

After the success of high-speed diesel railcars in Germany, the feasibility of a similar operation in Britain was considered by the LNER. Gresley found that steam locomotives could outperform the diesel railcars after trials with A1 and A3 Class engines. As the Silver Jubilee of King George V was approaching it was decided to introduce a high-speed service between Newcastle and London to commemorate the occasion. A new locomotive was to be constructed for this service and at first it was to be based on the P2 Class but this was abandoned and the new A4 was an improvement of the A3 Class. No. 2509 *Silver Link* was the first of the class to be built in September 1935 with a further three appearing before 1936. Thirty-one more engines had been built by mid-1938, all at Doncaster Works.

A4 No. 2509, 1935

Another view of Gresley's first A4 taken in 1935 when the locomotive was new. Apart from the striking design of the locomotive, the colour scheme employed on the first engines would have caught the eye as it was different to the standard green livery of the LNER passenger locomotives. No. 2509 *Silver Link* was painted in three shades of grey: dark charcoal at the front, battleship grey for the skirting and a silver grey for the boiler casing, tender and wheels. In this picture the silver grey runs all the way to the front of the sides of the locomotive but this was quickly changed to include the parabolic curve of dark charcoal on the sides, which became a distinguishing feature of the class. It also has its nameplates fitted though these were also quickly changed before entering full service. Its name was instead painted on the boiler casing in a central position (see the other photograph of No. 2509 *Silver Link*, which illustrates these changes).

A4 No. 2510, 1935

No. 2510 *Quicksilver* entered service in September 1935 three weeks after No. 2509 *Silver Link*. The first four A4 engines incorporated 'silver' in their name to complement the name of the 'Silver Jubilee' service. The regular service started at the end of September 1935, running Monday to Friday departing from Newcastle at 10 a.m. to arrive at King's Cross at 2 p.m. with only one stop at Darlington. The return left King's Cross at 5.30 p.m. to arrive at Newcastle at 9.30 p.m. *Quicksilver* went to work on the service after *Silver Link* had put in two weeks' unbroken service. The two locomotives and No. 2512 *Silver Fox* were allocated to King's Cross to operate the service while one, No. 2511 *Silver King*, was at Gateshead shed.

P2 No. 2006 (Streamlined), 1936

No. 2006 *Wolf of Badenoch* was built in September 1936 and was the last of the P2 Class to appear. It was built with front-end streamline casing similar to that of the A4 Class as were the previous three engines. The first two engines were similarly altered, No. 2002 in 1936 and No. 2001 in 1938. When built *Wolf of Badenoch* was fitted with a diagram 108 boiler instead of a diagram 106 fitted to the other P2s. In the diagram 108 boiler, the distance between the tubeplates was reduced and the firebox combustion chamber was increased by 1 foot in length. This boiler later went to No. 2002 *Earl Marischal* after it was rebuilt to A2/2, but was only retained for eighteen months. Thereafter the boiler was scrapped.

Above: **A3 No. 2750 with Dynamometer Car and Five Coaches, 1935**
As part of Gresley's investigation into the use of steam locomotives for a high-speed express service, two trials were made. One with A1 No. 4472 *Flying Scotsman* and the other with A3 No. 2750 *Papyrus*. After the first run with *Flying Scotsman* between London King's Cross and Leeds was quite successful a second run between the capital and Newcastle with *Papyrus* was scheduled for 5 March 1935. The train consisted of five coaches and the dynamometer car weighing 217 tons gross. The run to Newcastle was unspectacular and it was reached in just over 237 minutes. On the return journey between Grantham and Peterborough a maximum speed of 108 mph was reached (a record at the time) and an average speed of 105.4 mph recorded. The Peterborough to King's Cross section was completed in a record time of 62 minutes 6 seconds and the total time was improved from the down run to 231 minutes. No. 2750 *Papyrus* is pictured at Barkston, north of Grantham, on 18 April 1935 with a similar train formation to that of the record-breaking run.

Opposite page, bottom: **A4 No. 4496, c. 1936**
No. 4496 *Golden Shuttle* was built at Doncaster Works in September 1936. As it was intended this locomotive should work the 'West Riding Limited' service along with No. 4495 *Golden Fleece* they were both given names associated with the wool trade. No. 4496 only carried the name for nine years before it was renamed *Dwight D. Eisenhower* in September 1945 at London Marylebone station. As BR No. 60008 the locomotive was withdrawn in July 1963 and subsequently preserved at Doncaster Works for shipment to the National Railroad Museum at Green Bay, Wisconsin, where it has resided since. Five other A4 Class locomotives have been preserved: No. 4468 (BR 60022) *Mallard*, No. 4489 (BR 60010) *Dominion of Canada*, No. 4498 (60007) *Sir Nigel Gresley*, No. 4488 (BR 60009) *Union of South Africa* and No. 4464 (BR60019) *Bittern*.

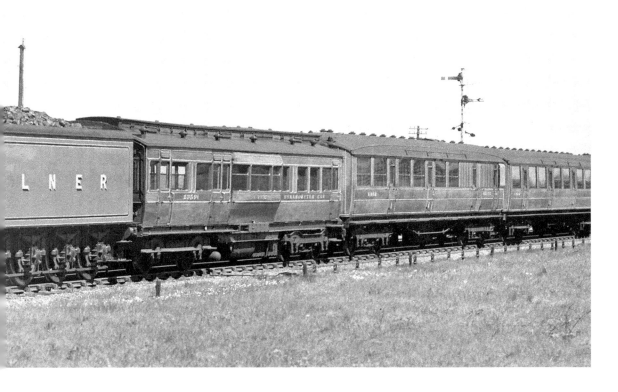

Above: **V2 Class No. 4772 Motion, 1936**
A close-up of the motion, which belonged to V2 Class No. 4772, taken on 24 August 1936. The V2 Class had three cylinders measuring 18½ inches by 26 inches with Walschaerts/Gresley motion and 9-inch piston valves, which were similar to those fitted to the A4 Class. When set at 65 per cent cut-off, the maximum valve travel was 5⅝ inches.

Above: **A3 No. 2796, 1930s**

Gresley Class A3 4-6-2 locomotive No. 2796, *Spearmint*, is pictured at the east end of No. 4 bay in the Crimpsall Repair Shop at Doncaster Works. It was built at the Works in May 1930. Before 1930 the Gresley Pacifics usually visited the main Works in the area they were allocated to for repairs and maintenance. After 1930 the sole responsibility for maintaining the A1s and A3s fell on Doncaster's shoulders. This lasted for thirty-three years until most were withdrawn and the introduction of diesels was in full swing. After 1963 the responsibility was given to Darlington.

Opposite page, bottom: **V2 No. 4771, 1936**

After much deliberation over the design of the new V2 Class locomotives, the first one, No. 4771 *Green Arrow*, emerged from Doncaster Works in June 1936. The engine was named after the newly-introduced registered goods service, which it was intended to work along with other services. Four further engines were constructed at Doncaster in 1936 before Darlington Works began contributing further members of the class from July 1937. In total 184 locomotives were produced at both Works, the last one entering service in July 1944.

Above: **A4 No. 4498 with Gresley,** *c.* **1937**
A4 No. 4498 was built at Doncaster Works in November 1937 and was the 100th Gresley Pacific to be built. After a suggestion by a member of the Railway Correspondence & Travel Society, this milestone was commemorated by naming the locomotive *Sir Nigel Gresley*. The locomotive is pictured at King's Cross shed with Sir Nigel Gresley.

Opposite page, bottom: **W1 No. 10000, 1937**
This picture of W1 Class 4-6-4 No. 10000 was taken in October 1937 after it had been rebuilt. The locomotive entered service to King's Cross but initial teething problems forced a reallocation to Doncaster in February 1938. In March 1939 it was back at King's Cross and working main line passenger services. A short spell at Haymarket came in 1942 before returning to King's Cross for the rest of the 1940s. In June 1948 it was given BR No. 60700. Final allocation to Doncaster came in October 1953.

Above: **B17 No. 2859, Late 1930s**
Locomotive No. 2859 *East Anglian* was originally built at Darlington in June 1936 as B17/4 Class and named *Norwich City*. It was streamlined in September 1937 at Doncaster Works. It is pictured there in No. 2 bay in the Crimpsall Repair Shop. No. 2859 was originally attached to the group standard 4,200-gallon tender but this was also modified to resemble the appearance of the streamlined tenders.

Above: **A4 No. 4492 and Coronation Train, 1937**
A4 No. 4492 *Dominion of New Zealand* is pictured at Retford in July 1937 hauling the Coronation train. The train left King's Cross at 4 p.m. and expected to pass York at 6.37 p.m. From York to Edinburgh the journey was expected to take 3 hours 20 minutes. Departing from Edinburgh at 4.30 p.m., the Up service stopped at Newcastle and was timed to arrive at King's Cross at 10.30 p.m. The service was worked by engines allocated to King's Cross and Edinburgh Haymarket sheds, with No. 4492 mainly at King's Cross during the service's operation though it did have an eight-month spell at Haymarket between July 1937 and March 1938. *Dominion of New Zealand* was also a noted performer on the 'Flying Scotsman' service after it was given to the A4s in 1937, running fifty-two consecutive trips and sixty-two overall. The 'Coronation' service ran for the last time on 31 August 1939.

Opposite page, bottom: **B17/5 No. 2870 Streamlined, 1937**
September 1937 saw B17/5 Class 4-6-0 No. 2870 *City of London* pose for its official photograph after being streamlined at Doncaster Works. The locomotive was originally built by R. Stephenson & Co. in May 1937 as *Manchester City*. The next engine, No. 2871, was to be named *Tottenham Hotspur* at a rolling stock exhibition, however the engine was not yet completed and the switching of the names occurred as No. 2870 was sent instead. No. 2870 *Tottenham Hotspur* and No. 2859 *Norwich City* were chosen to operate the East Anglian service because these football teams were at either end of the journey. Both were in service with streamlining for fourteen years before it was removed at Gorton Works in April 1951 and they reverted to their original appearance. No. 2870 was withdrawn as BR No. 61670 in April 1960.

Above: **V2 Monobloc Casting,** *c.* **1930s**
Employees are pictured working with the monobloc cylinder for a V2 Class locomotive after it has been cast in a mould. The arrangement of the cylinders in this manner was at first advantageous as it reduced steam leakage and was lighter than the normal arrangement. Later, however, problems arose if cracks appeared in the casting as a repair or replacement was a time-consuming and expensive process. To resolve the problem it was decided to fit separate cylinders to make repairs and replacement easier.

Opposite page, bottom: **C1 No. 3279, 1938**
This Ivatt C1 Atlantic is pictured after being rebuilt at Doncaster Works in June 1938. The engine, No. 3279, was originally erected at the Works in June 1904 as GNR No. 279 with two cylinders and Stephenson slide valves. It was rebuilt by Gresley in 1915 with four cylinders measuring 16½ inches by 26 inches, later reduced to 15 inches by 26 inches, with Walschaerts valve gear. In 1938 the rebuild brought it back to two cylinders with 10-inch piston valves with Walschaerts valve gear and a larger cab, seen here, after Gresley objected to the retention of the smaller cab when originally completed at the end of April. February 1948 saw the locomotive leave service.

Above: **P2 No. 2003, 1938**

P2 Class No. 2003, *Lord President*, is pictured undergoing a general repair at Doncaster Works on 3 April 1938. The repairs had started on 11 March and would last until 9 April when the locomotive went back to traffic. This was the first general repair for the locomotive since entering service in June 1936. Three visits had been paid to Cowlairs Works for light repairs between 1936 and 1937. September 1944 saw the locomotive enter Doncaster Works to be rebuilt by Thompson and become part of the A2/2 Class.

Above: **Corridor Tender Alteration, 1938**

When entering service the first members of the A4 Class were equipped with a new corridor tender, which was an updated version of the ones fitted to the A1 and A3 classes. As more A4 engines were being ordered it was decided to attach them with the 1928 corridor tenders after the tenders had been refurbished. As part of the alterations, plating was fitted to the top of the tenders, which reduced the coal capacity. While working the 'Coronation' service it was found that the engine was running out of coal before the end of the journey. Thus, it was decided the plating should be removed so more coal could be carried, which is what this photograph is depicting during March 1938. The tender is No. 5328 and it was carried behind No. 4489 *Dominion of Canada* between December 1937 and June 1953 and August 1953 and August 1960.

Opposite page, bottom: **A1 No. 2547, 1939**

No. 2547 *Doncaster* is pictured after completing a general repair in July 1939. The locomotive was built in August 1924 at Doncaster but it did not take its name from the Works which contributed so many members of the class. It was the name of the racehorse that won the 1873 Derby. The locomotive was allocated to Doncaster shed a number of times during its career, the longest being thirteen years and four months between October 1935 and February 1949 before moving to Leicester. *Doncaster* was rebuilt to A3 in May 1946 and was withdrawn in September 1963 and scrapped at Doncaster.

Above: **V1 Class No. 447, October 1938**

No. 447, a V1 Class 2-6-2T locomotive, was the first of twelve engines in the class to be fitted with Westinghouse brakes and vacuum ejectors. This was fitted for use on suburban services that departed from London Liverpool Street station to places such as Clacton, Hertford and Witham. The V1s were replaced on these services by L1 Class locomotives and were later transferred to Scotland and the North East. The Westinghouse equipment was subsequently removed on these twelve engines and No. 447 underwent the change in June 1955, one of the last of the class to do so. It was removed from service in August 1962.

Foundry Worker, 1941
A smith at a fire in Doncaster Works poses for the camera on 15 May 1941. The picture was one of six taken at the site for use by Doncaster art students.

Class O2/3 No. 3833, *c.* 1942
Class O2/3 2-8-0 No. 3833 was the first of the final batch of 25 O2 Class locomotives to be constructed, all at Doncaster Works, between 1942 and 1943. Few modifications were made to these engines from the previous batch built between 1932 and 1934, but the modifications that were made included vacuum brakes for the locomotive and the tender, improved superheater arrangement and the increase in diameter of the axle journals to 8¾ inches. Due to the shortage of material during the war, the locomotive was attached to a 4,200-gallon group standard tender from a D49 Class locomotive. No. 3833 left service as BR No. 63965 in September 1963.

Second World War, 1943

A scene in D6 shop showing the construction of naval guns and the frame for a locomotive. During the Second World War, Doncaster Works carried out war work in conjunction with building and repairing locomotives. The photograph was one of three taken on 4 September 1943.

A4 No. 4466, 1944

Posing for the camera on 4 January 1944 is Gresley A4 Pacific No. 4466, *Sir Ralph Wedgwood*. The locomotive was originally named *Herring Gull* when it entered service in January 1938. The change came about as the locomotive, which originally carried the name of the chief general manager, was damaged beyond repair after an air raid at York on 29 April 1942. No. 4466 is about to leave Doncaster Works after a general repair that started on 1 December 1943. As well as the name change it had the cut-off increased to 75 per cent and it looks like a new coat of paint has been applied. Black was applied to locomotives during the Second World War and it had initially been applied to No. 4466 in February 1942.

Bruce Woodcock, 1945
Pictured undertaking boiler
work is Bruce Woodcock, fitter,
on 1 August 1945. He was
also a champion boxer holding
the British, British Empire and
European heavyweight titles in the
latter half of the 1940s.

A2/2 No. 2006, 1944
Photographed on 12 April 1944 is former Gresley P2 Class 2-8-2 locomotive No. 2006 *Wolf of Badenoch*, which was rebuilt by Thompson as an A2, later A2/2 Class engine. The P2s, while in service in Scotland, experienced problems due to the difficult nature of the track they operated on between Edinburgh and Aberdeen. Ironically they had been specifically designed to overcome the problems caused by this track. Suitable work could have been found for them elsewhere, however Thompson's solution to their problems was total rebuilding to a 4-6-2 wheel configuration. Other changes included 20-inch cylinders, 10-inch piston valves, three separate sets of motion replacing the Gresley arrangement, shortened boiler length, Kylchap double blastpipe and chimney with wing-type smoke deflectors and increased cut-off to 75 per cent. All six P2s had been rebuilt by the end of 1944.

Main Machine Shop, 1945

Mr H. Stanley Richards is pictured on 4 October 1945 in the Main Machine Shop (D Shop) operating a cylinder-boring machine.

A1/1 No. 4470, 1945

On 19 September 1945 No. 4470 *Great Northern*, the pioneer Gresley A1 Class Pacific, is pictured after it was completely rebuilt by Thompson. This engine bore little resemblance to the one that had entered Doncaster Works on 1 May 1945. The alterations included new frames, new cylinder arrangement, three separate sets of Walschaerts valve gear, A4 Class diagram 107 boiler, short cab sides, Kylchap double blastpipe and chimney and a cut-off increased to 75 per cent. The merits of this conversion, especially the choice of engine, are well documented elsewhere but it is worth noting that the engine in its rebuilt form was certainly capable of some good performances. Plans were in place to rebuild the remaining A1 Class locomotives (then A10s) to the specifications of *Great Northern*, however they were rebuilt as A3 instead. No. 4470 was taken out of service as BR No. 60113 in November 1962.

L1 No. 9000 Cab and Locomotive, 1945

Two views of Thompson L1 Class 2-6-4T No. 9000 taken during May 1945. No. 9000 was the prototype engine of the class and was the first new design of locomotive to be built at Doncaster after the end of the Second World War. It was also the only one of the class to enter service for the LNER as the rest came into service between 1948 and 1950 for BR. Ninety-nine other locomotives were built at Darlington, North British Locomotive Co. and R. Stephenson, Hawthorns. No. 9000 was the only one to be built at Doncaster. The L1s were designed for suburban passenger services to replace A5, N2 and N5 Class locomotives. No. 9000 performed an extended period of trials between entering service and 1947, undertaking a large variety of duties. It was found to be a very competent engine, beating the performance of many engines tested against it. The main problem found in the trials was that with heavy loads and adverse gradients the engine's brakes were totally inadequate. The cab was found to be too draughty when the class was in service and this necessitated the fitting of full-length doors with drop-down windows to the cabs of each engine. No. 9000 was withdrawn in December 1960 and the last member of the class left service two years later.

A2/3 No. 500, 1946

New Pacific locomotives were authorised in 1944 and they were to be built to Edward Thompson's standardised design. Thirty were ordered but only fifteen were built and the rest were redesigned and became Peppercorn A2s. The A2/3s were largely based on the A2/2s which were rebuilt Gresley P2 2-8-2 locomotives. The A2/3s had 19-inch diameter cylinders, fully-sloping firebox grate, a 6-foot 5-inch diameter boiler with a pressure of 250 lbs per square inch and large type smoke deflectors. No. 500 *Edward Thompson*, named after the designer as he was retiring as chief mechanical engineer, was the first to be built and entered service in May 1946. It left service as BR No. 60500 in June 1963.

This picture was one of a number taken in November 1942 illustrating women on war work at Doncaster Works. This particular picture was titled 'Drop Hammer Driver'.

K1/1 No. 3445, 1946

This locomotive, No. 3445 *MacCailin Mór*, was originally built at Darlington Works in January 1939 as a Gresley K4 Class 2-6-0 locomotive. In March 1945 the locomotive entered Doncaster Works and was rebuilt to Thompson's specifications. This included reducing the number of cylinders from three to two and fitting a redesigned pony truck, and a new diagram 116 boiler, based on the B1 Class diagram 100A, was also installed. The engine was classified K1, later K1/1, and was the only K4 to be rebuilt. New locomotives were built instead to these specifications (slightly modified by Peppercorn) and were ordered in 1947. Built by the North British Locomotive Co. between 1949 and 1950 the K1 Class (including No. 3445) eventually totalled seventy-one. No. 3445, as BR No. 61997, was taken out of service in June 1961.

LNER Men, *c.* 1946

George Wilson, in the cab, is seen on the last day of his fifty years' railway service. Driver E. Hine of Leeds is also pictured. Both men are posing for the camera with No. 46 *Diamond Jubilee*. The picture dates from after July 1946 and before BR number 60046 was applied. The locomotive was built at Doncaster in August 1924 and was given LNER No. 2545. It left service in June 1963.

A4 No. 4468 with Group, 1940s

Gresley A4 Pacific No. 4468 *Mallard* is pictured with a group of premium apprentices during August/September 1943 and they are David Sandiland (on loco), then, from left to right, Peter Townend, Bill Taylor, Jack Taylor, Harry Steel, Alan Coggon and Dick Hardy. The locomotive was built at Doncaster Works during March 1938 and was the first A4 to be built with a Kylchap double blastpipe and chimney. *Mallard* had a relatively small number of allocations, the first being at Doncaster until moving to Grantham in October 1943. The next and final move was to King's Cross in April 1948. Withdrawal came fifteen years later in April 1963. Photo reproduced courtesy of Dick Hardy.

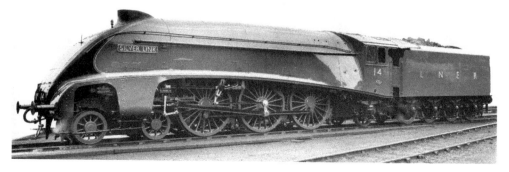

A4 No. 14, 1946

After the end of the Second World War it was decided that the livery of the A4s would revert back to the pre-war garter blue. The first to be repainted was No. 2509 *Silver Link*. The work was carried out at Doncaster Works prior to this photograph being taken on 13 June 1946. It had entered the Works for light repairs on 22 May and left on 14 June. Also, while it was there, *Silver Link* was renumbered 14 as part of the renumbering scheme. It was also refitted with metal numbers on the cab and LNER letters on the tender.

Peppercorn A2 No. 525 and Group, 1947

After Edward Thompson's retirement in 1946, Arthur Henry Peppercorn became the last Chief Mechanical Engineer of the LNER. It was quickly decided that fifteen A2/3 engines on order were to have their design revised and be built in a more conventional manner. This included moving

the bogie so the outside cylinders were positioned between the wheels. No. 525 *A. H. Peppercorn* was the only Peppercorn A2 to be built for the LNER; the remaining fourteen appeared after nationalisation. The locomotive is pictured on the last day of the LNER, 31 December 1947, with its designer (front row, centre) and other Doncaster staff adjacent to the Crimpsall Repair Shop.

Bibliography

Butt, R. V. J., *The Directory of Railway Stations* (1995)

Grafton, Peter, *Edward Thompson of the LNER* (2007)

Griffiths, Roger and John Hooper, *Great Northern Railway Engine Sheds Volume 3: Yorkshire and Lancashire* (2000)

Groves. N., *Great Northern Locomotive History Volume 1: 1847–1866* (1986)

Groves. N., *Great Northern Locomotive History Volume 2: 1867–1895 The Stirling Era* (1991)

Groves. N., *Great Northern Locomotive History Volume 3A: 1896–1911 The Ivatt Era* (1990)

Groves. N., *Great Northern Locomotive History Volume 3B: 1911–1922 The Gresley Era* (1992)

Harris, Michael, *Gresley's Coaches: Coaches Built for the GNR, ECJS and LNER 1905–1953* (1973)

Harris, Michael, *LNER Carriages* (2011)

Hoole, Ken, *The Illustrated History of East Coast Joint Stock* (1993)

RCTS, *Locomotives of the LNER: Part 1 Preliminary Survey* (1963)

RCTS, *Locomotives of the LNER: Part 2A Tender Engines – Classes A1 to A10* (1978)

RCTS, *Locomotives of the LNER: Part 2B Tender Engines – Classes B1 to B19* (1975)

RCTS, *Locomotives of the LNER: Part 3A Tender Engines – Classes C1 to C11* (1979)

RCTS, *Locomotives of the LNER: Part 3B Tender Engines – Classes D1 to 12* (1980)

RCTS, *Locomotives of the LNER: Part 3C Tender Engines – Classes D13 to D24* (1981)

RCTS, *Locomotives of the LNER: Part 4 Tender Engines – Classes D25 to E7* (1968)

RCTS, *Locomotives of the LNER: Part 5 Tender Engines – Classes J1 to J37* (1984)

RCTS, *Locomotives of the LNER: Part 6A Tender Engines – Classes J38 to K5* (1982)

RCTS, *Locomotives of the LNER: Part 6B Tender Engines – Classes O1 to P2* (1991)

RCTS, *Locomotives of the LNER: Part 6C Tender Engines – Classes Q1 to Y10* (1984)

RCTS, *Locomotives of the LNER: Part 7 Tank Engines – Classes A5 to H2* (1991)

RCTS, *Locomotives of the LNER: Part 8A Tank Engines – Classes J50 to J70* (1970)

RCTS, *Locomotives of the LNER: Part 8B Tank Engines – Class J71 to J94* (1971)

RCTS, *Locomotives of the LNER: Part 9A Tank Engines – Classes L1 to N19* (1977)

RCTS, *Locomotives of the LNER: Part 9B Tank Engines – Classes Q1 to Z5* (1977)

RCTS, *Locomotives of the LNER: Part 10A Departmental Stock, Locomotive Sheds, Boiler and Tender Numbering* (1991)

Wrottesley, John, *The Great Northern Railway Volume 1: Origins and Development* (1979)

Wrottesley, John, *The Great Northern Railway Volume 2: Expansion and Competition* (1979)

Wrottesley, John, *The Great Northern Railway Volume 3: Twentieth Century to Grouping* (1981)

Yeadon, W. B., *Yeadon's Register of LNER Locomotives Volume One: Gresley A1 and A3 Classes* (2001)

Yeadon, W. B., *Yeadon's Register of LNER Locomotives Volume Two: Gresley A4 and W1 Classes* (2001)

Yeadon, W. B., *Yeadon's Register of LNER Locomotives Volume Three: Raven, Thompson and Peppercorn Pacifics* (2001)

Yeadon, W. B., *Yeadon's Register of LNER Locomotives Volume Four: Gresley V2 and V4 Classes* (2001)